Shakespeare on Theatre

...On Theatre Series

*What the world's greatest dramatists
had to say about theatre, in their own words*

Chekhov on Theatre

compiled by Jutta Hercher *and* Peter Urban
translated by Stephen Mulrine

Shakespeare on Theatre

edited by Nick de Somogyi

Shakespeare on Theatre

edited by
Nick de Somogyi

NICK HERN BOOKS
London
www.nickhernbooks.co.uk

A NICK HERN BOOK

Shakespeare on Theatre
first published in Great Britain in 2012
by Nick Hern Books Limited,
14 Larden Road, London W3 7ST

The drawing of the Swan Theatre on p. 113
is courtesy of World History Archive/TopFoto

Cover illustration by Nick de Somogyi
Cover design by www.energydesignstudio.com

Typeset by Nick Hern Books, London
Printed and bound in Great Britain by
Ashford Colour Press, Gosport, Hampshire

A CIP catalogue record for this book
is available from the British Library

ISBN 978 1 84842 079 3

in memoriam

GEOFFREY BURNSTONE

(1925–2009)

Contents

The world's a Theatre: the earth a stage,
Plac'd in the midst, where both the prince and page,
Both rich and poor, fool, wise man, base and high,
All act their parts in life's short Tragedy.
Our life's a tragedy: those secret rooms
Wherein we tire us are our mothers' wombs.
The music ush'ring in the play is mirth
To see a man-child brought upon the earth.
That fainting gasp of breath which first we vent
Is a Dumb Show; presents the argument.
Our new-born cries, that new-born griefs bewray,
Are the sad Prologue of th'ensuing play.
False hopes, true fears, vain joys, and fierce distracts
Are like the music that divides the Acts.
Time holds the glass, and when the hour's outrun,
Death strikes the Epilogue, and the Play is done.

Francis Quarles, 'On the Life
and Death of a Man' (c. 1630)

Introduction

1 ACTOR. Gods of the theater, smile on us.
2 ACTOR. You who sit up there, stern in judgment,
    Smile on us.
1 ACTOR. You who look down on actors—
BOTH. And who doesn't?

Stephen Sondheim (1974)

Whatever else he was or wasn't – and bookshelves groan with contending theories – William Shakespeare (1564–1616) was a working man of the theatre to his core. If, to quote the maxim he perfected, 'All the world's a stage… And one man in his time plays many parts', then the world of the theatre in which he lived and worked supplied him with a lifetime of roles. The stage-struck boy, watching in wonder the outlandish spectacle of touring productions. The young father drawn to the amateur dramatics of local maygames and revels. Then, talent-spotted by a later touring troupe, the industrious jobbing actor, hitching his fortunes to the grinding wagon of provincial rep, and learning the tricks of this gradually lucrative trade. Next, in step with his growing confidence as an actor, his precociously impressive skills as a textual fixer for the increasingly creaky melodramas of the repertoire – an improviser of verse and plot no less impressive than the showier repartee of the company Clown. In time, of course, the Londoner, and – after sharing the modern duties of dramaturg, prompter, and ASM – another new title to go with his burgeoning success as a junior co-author: 'upstart'. Despite being disparaged by the Oxbridge élite in 1592 as a provincial jack of all trades, 'as well able to bombast out a blank verse as the best' of them, Shakespeare's parts proliferated: bestselling love-poet (1593); founder-member, with the actor Richard Burbage and the clown Will Kemp, of the Lord Chamberlain's Men (1594); published – and publicized – playwright (1598); shareholder and artistic director at the Globe theatre (1599); 'the best and chiefest of our modern writers' (1601); principal dramatist of the King's Men, and celebrity box-office gold (1603); financial and artistic investor in the Blackfriars theatre (1609); senior co-author, mentor, and consultant (1613–14); and eventually, after a lifetime spent in a profession legally defined as little better than that of 'rogues and vagabonds', the part he may have cherished most, the one with which he described himself in his will (1616): 'gentleman'. But when, in 1602, an officer at the College of Heralds expressed doubt over Shakespeare's right to his coat of arms, the condescending term he used probably in fact best defines the man's lifelong rank, profession, or occupation: 'Shakespear yᵉ Player'.

Shakespeare was a 'player' in nearly all the definitions available in the *Oxford English Dictionary* (*OED*) – 'gambler', 'competitive contestant', 'professional (as opposed to gentleman)', 'financial speculator', 'sexually successful individual', 'respected, or influential person' – but chiefly, of course, in the specifically theatrical sense that enabled all the others throughout his lifetime: 'A person who acts a character on the stage; a dramatic performer, an actor.' From the late 1580s to the early 1610s, Shakespeare's life was regulated by the demands made on him as a 'dramatic performer'. His calendar years were divided into theatrical seasons, themselves irregularly organized (by politics or plague) between London's playhouses, its various aristocratic households, and the slog of provincial touring. The odd month or so was presumably snatched back home in Stratford, but his London weeks were determined by an exhausting schedule of all-but daily performance, whether for public profit at the theatre, or private reward at court. The diary of his London days was principally governed by the demands of the public theatres in which he worked – the Theater, the Curtain, the Rose, and the Globe –

where, open to the skies, performances largely depended on daylight, the three hours or so of their typical duration therefore starting at around two o'clock in the afternoon. (The candle-light of the indoor Blackfriars theatre was later to extend the available playing time, for a richer clientele, into dark winter afternoons and evenings.)

The rival public theatres seem to have competed for their trade by presenting a different, often new, play every day (while regularly rotating performances of the staple favourites) – a schedule that must have dictated a punishing régime for its actors. With his afternoons devoted to performance, Shakespeare's mornings must often have involved group rehearsals on the unattended stage – sorting out a new play's blocking, for example, rehearsing its duels, dances, battles, and special effects, or else simply refreshing the collective memory of an earlier production required for its revival that afternoon. Days were long, and those evenings that were free from the demands of private performance at court or elsewhere would presumably have been as much taken up with the constant grind of learning lines – and in Shakespeare's case writing and revising them – as the riotous boozing and wenching of popular imagination. Playing was – as it has always been – extremely hard work.

Modern playwrights have increasingly taken to donating (or selling) their working papers to the world's great libraries, where future scholars may pore over the drafts, rewrites, notes, bills, invoices, and practical correspondence relating to the day-to-day business of making theatre. As it happens, the greatest precedent for such a bequest precisely dates from a few months after Shakespeare's death, when the charitable foundation established at Dulwich by Burbage's great rival, the actor Edward Alleyn, first began its work. To this day, the busy transactions of an Elizabethan theatre (the Rose), recorded in the so-called 'Diary' of its manager (Alleyn's father-in-law) Philip Henslowe, together with a rich mass of manuscript correspondence, remains secure in the archives of Dulwich College. The nearest Shakespeare ever came to bequeathing the 'dedicated words which writers use / Of their fair subject' (Sonnet 82), however, was the deposit at Oxford's Bodleian Library of a copy of the 1623 First Folio, the posthumously collected edition of his plays prepared by two of his 'fellows', John Heminge and Henry Condell.

In the absence, therefore, of any private, backstage commentary by the world's foremost playwright – and unlike the other inaugural title in this series, *Chekhov on Theatre* – this anthology of *Shakespeare on Theatre* necessarily depends on the public, published nature of his surviving works. Those works, furthermore, seem almost perversely to have steered away from any direct depiction of the London theatre-land in which they were first written and performed. Unlike the many colleagues with whom he worked, collaborated, or quarrelled – Jonson, Marston, and Middleton spring immediately to mind – Shakespeare seems to have winced from dramatizing the daily business of his life too closely. At the same time, the amdram tantrums of the 'mechanicals' in *A Midsummer Night's Dream* (1595), the notably incompetent pageant that concludes *Love's Labour's Lost* (1595), and the troupes of strolling players that transform the stages of *The Taming of the Shrew* (1592) and *Hamlet* (1600–1), for example, cannot but reflect insights into his own profession. Necessarily oblique though such extended glimpses are, however, it does not take very long for a reader or performer of his plays to realize how often his characters 'talk shop' by incorporating the technical vocabulary of the stage – the nuts, bolts, and nitty-gritty of their actor–author's craft. Whether in the relish with which Richard of Gloucester raids the props-basket, the impatience Othello barks at a premature prompt, or the anxious interpretation Bassanio places on an appreciative audience, Shakespeare drew repeated inspiration from the daily circumstances of his working life, almost as if unbidden to his mind.

That inspiration was further assisted by the deeply felt and widespread contemporary notion that each of our individual human lives comprises but a brief cameo appearance in (what Ralegh called) 'this stage-play world'. Shakespeare's variant of that phrase – 'All the world's a stage' – has become a commonplace of modern quotation, but the premise it summarized was everywhere in the culture that gave rise to it. The theatrical sense of life, from the trumpeting of its 'crying' entrance to its inevitable exit – 'curtains', as we still say – profoundly influenced the way it was conducted, from the highest spectacle of monarchy to the daily squalid display of public execution. (The two extremes of this commonplace were to be shockingly conflated in 1649, when Charles I was beheaded outside the building originally designed as an indoor theatre for his father.) At a time when the complex hierarchy of 'sumptuary law' minutely regulated who was allowed to wear what, when, and why – and when theatre companies routinely spent more on lavish costumes for a new production than was paid to the authors for its script – the business of the stage, or scaffold, was the material of life.

Drawn from the thirty-six plays collected in the definitive First Folio, as well as the poems and the handful of further plays not included there, and supplemented by reference to the – sometimes dramatically – different wording of their Quarto texts, *Shakespeare on Theatre* seeks to identify, extract, and present the observations of a lifetime spent on the stage. In addition, since by its nature Shakespeare's theatrical career throughout involved and required active collaboration, a range of material by his contemporaries has also been included. These supplementary extracts always engage directly with his own words and works, whether in deliberate reply, contemporary parallel, eye-witness observation, or later memory, or else from passages in works to which he is known to have contributed – most prominently the multi-authored *Sir Thomas More* (in which another troupe of strolling players perform for its title-hero).

The structure of *Shakespeare on Theatre* broadly follows the progress of a play's 'Jacobethan' production. After a Prologue announcing the tactics by which, in the days before proscenium curtains or blackouts, his audiences were invited to exchange reality for fiction, there come three sections detailing the practical run-up to performance: from (the equivalents of) the audition-hall, via the rehearsal-room, to the costume-

XV

department. In keeping with the practical nature of the collection – and in illustration of the ways in which the print of surviving play-texts can sometimes distort or disguise the complicated processes by which they came about – we also include a 'definitive' text of Peter Quince's *Pyramus and Thisbe* (the play-within-the-play featured in *A Midsummer Night's Dream*). The next three sections are concerned with the fate of a production from the moment its cast first tread the boards of their theatre – a theatre whose character, structure, and symbolism differed, often profoundly, from our own. But some theatrical experiences endure unchanged, whether in the shape of a fluffed line, a missed cue, or the love–hate relationship that exists between an actor and his audience. ('*His* audience' because in Shakespeare's day all actors were male – hence the detailed instructions he supplies to the boy-actors playing his female leads.) The fact that Shakespeare and his fellows occasionally grovelled to their royal or aristocratic patrons in their courts, while frequently – and literally – looking down their noses at the groundlings in their public theatre-yards, perhaps represents another continuity for a profession that has always, in Francis Quarles's phrase, been uniquely 'Plac'd in the midst'. Quarles's take on the theatre of our lives (which supplies the epigraph to this book) is one in a series of versions of that theme supplied here – as much as anything to demonstrate Shakespeare's characteristic perfection of what was then already a cliché. The final section of *Shakespeare on Theatre* supplies an Epilogue suggesting the various ways in which a performance can live on in the mind after those inevitable final words, in theatre as in life, 'You that way; we this way'.

Shakespeare seems to have been the first actor in England to be more or less directly described as a 'Thespian' (see below, p. 185). The roles he actually learned and played on the various stages of his career include parts in satirical Comedies and classical Tragedies (according to the cast-lists Ben Jonson supplied for *Every Man in His Humour* and *Sejanus*), as well as the 'kingly parts' of History plays. A later tradition associates him with 'old man' characters (perhaps because of his baldness), and it is increasingly accepted that he may also have débuted many of his own Choruses. The shape and span of that career, from bit-part spear-carrier to distinguished mentor, set him apart from most of his rivals. Educated at university or the Inns of Court, those gentleman-playwrights may have trumped his knowledge of Latin and Greek, but they lacked his hands-on experience of theatre's daily graft. The material gathered in this book therefore ranges from an early tip about how to provoke onstage tears by using an onion-soaked handkerchief, to his grandest reflections on the relation of art to life. It is in part because Shakespeare knew what it was to feel his mouth go dry, and to sense that brief tremor in his limbs as he walked onstage, that the words he wrote have lasted so freshly and vividly into an age when performances are regularly 'blue-screened', 'digitally enhanced', or 'phoned in'. The 'message' of Shakespeare's plays will endlessly change, but their 'medium' will last for as long as human beings continue to tell each other stories on a stage.

All the extracts collected below have been modernized from their early modern spellings and punctuation, and follow the conventions established in the ongoing 'Shakespeare Folios' series (NHB, 2000—). Quotation from Shakespeare's plays generally follows the 1623 Folio, though the wording from earlier Quarto editions is sometimes also selected. The years supplied for each extract refer to their respective play's likeliest first performance, or in the case of poems and prose to their date of publication. The individual Section Introductions seek to explain and contextualize the material included in each, while additional explanations also preface many of the individual extracts. The alphabetical Glossary at the end of the book (pp. 189–206) is intended to explain the often difficult words and allusions used in the main text, where they are cued by a °preceding 'degree'-symbol. Extracts by authors other than Shakespeare have been set in a different style of type, and have also been modernized, by the present editor, where necessary.

    This book is based on an original idea by Nick Hern, and I remain deeply grateful to him, both for his continuing faith in me, and for his unparalleled editorial judgement. Profound thanks are also due to the patiently brilliant expertise of Matt Applewhite, Robin Booth, Jodi Gray, and Ian Higham at NHB, as also to the many other friends who have variously helped it on its way, chief among them Fiona Brannon, Dan Burnstone, Miles Croally, Georgina Difford, Calista Lucy, Jane Maud, Jan and Cas Piggott, Tim Underhill, Peter White, and Mary Wilmer.

Prologues and Inductions

Like hungry guests a sitting audience looks,
Plays are like suppers: poets are their cooks.
The founders you; the table is this place:
The carvers we; the Prologue is the grace.

Peter Motteux (1702)

A Prologue to a play is out of date,
A leisurely technique of masquerade.
So please regard me as a friendly shade,
Returning down the years to indicate,
More by my presence than by what I say,
The atmosphere and setting of this play.

Noël Coward (1951)

'Open your ears!' The first words of the Chorus to Shakespeare's *Henry IV, Part Two* (1597) may not seem very subtle, but they are effective. Spoken by the complex figure of 'Rumour', his costume 'painted full of tongues', they demand a receptive silence from the chattering audience – 'the blunt monster with uncounted heads' he calls them – now gathered in the open yard before him, and in the echo-chamber of the surrounding galleries. 'Shut your mouths!' is what he doesn't say, but what he certainly means; 'Open your ears!' – to a theatre then essentially reliant for its scenery, atmosphere, and lighting on the power of the spoken word. These days on London's South Bank, the National Theatre publicly flags its repertoire on an electronic billboard outside, ushers its audiences to their seats via a PA system counting down the minutes to curtain-up, and typically signals the outset of each production by dimming the house lights – thereby curtailing the mass perusal of an expensively printed programme, silencing small-talk, and directing all expectant eyes to the pitch-black stage before of them.* Needless to say, none of these technical resources was available to the theatres in which Shakespeare worked, though the same practical requirements still held – 'As happy prologues to the swelling act' (*Macbeth*, 1.3).

Four centuries ago, flyers for forthcoming attractions at the public playhouses would be commissioned from a local printer, and posted about town a day or so in advance. Flags – bearing the theatre's emblem (or logo) – would be run up the flag-poles to announce an afternoon's playing. As the audience gathered, a trumpeter would sound a flourish for the ten-minute call, then a second blast to hurry lingerers along, before a third 'sounding' announced the imminent performance itself. It was natural light that largely determined the running-time of plays (whether in the early inn-yards or the open-air the-atres later modelled on them); and even when it didn't – for those productions performed indoors in the great halls of aris-tocratic households, or in the commercial private theatres – mere candlepower alone simply couldn't stretch to a modern 'blackout'. And so, in both cases, some sort of music had always supplied the obvious means by which to silence a seated audience's social chatter, and summon their attention to the stage (much as a modern musical settles an audience by the striking up of its 'overture' by the band).

Indoor performances had long begun with an elaborately mimed sequence of action, to musical accompaniment, that would summarize the plot or symbolic moral of the play (or section of the play) it introduced, as well as setting the appro-priate mood. The early Elizabethan tragedy *Gorboduc* (1560) typically prefaced each of its acts with just such a 'Dumb Show' – choreographed to a series of suitably different instruments (violins, cornets, flutes, woodwind 'hautboys', and drums),

---

* As Peter Hall nicely puts it, 'Gas and then electric light made darkness possible' (*The Necessary Theatre* (Nick Hern Books, 1999), p. 14).

each of which was attuned to the themes they introduced (discord, royalty, mourning, ghostliness, and war). By the time Shakespeare started out in the theatre, in the late 1580s, such a convention had begun to feel old-fashioned – though the format remained vivid in his imagination. It is something of a black joke, for example, that the garden-scene in *Henry VI, Part One* (1592), in which the Yorkist and Lancastrian factions pluck the white and red flowers as their respective emblems, is cued by Plantagenet's command, 'Since you are tongue-tied and so loath to speak, / In dumb significants proclaim your thoughts' (2.4): curtain-up on the catastrophic civil war known as the Wars of the Roses. The most famous example of this antiquated device remains the detailed Dumb Show prefacing Prince Hamlet's court production of *The Murder of Gonzago* at Elsinore (see below, pp. 15–16) – though that elaborately mimed play-within-the-play-within-the-play might just as well have served, to an earlier theatrical generation, as a scene-setter for *Hamlet* itself.

As things turn out there (and aptly for a play so endlessly preoccupied with delay), the Dumb Show to *The Murder of Gonzago*, unlike those in *Gorboduc*, is succeeded, not by any action, but by the entrance of the figure that had superseded it in the public theatres: the Prologue. Some sense of that early theatrical transition, from Dumb Show to Prologue, survives into the 'war of looks' Shakespeare describes between the amorous goddess Venus and Adonis, the reluctant object of her desires, in his 1593 poem of that name. Studiedly avoiding her penetrating gaze, and in a pantomime of evasion, we read that 'all this dumb play had his acts made plain / With tears which chorus-like her eyes did rain': the protracted Dumb Show of his rejection prompts the more dramatic effect of her tearful Chorus.

It has been estimated that around half the plays written in the period feature a Prologue, Chorus, or Epilogue (a Classical device already venerable by the time Shakespeare began his career) – though it may well be that many more such speeches were written and performed than have survived attached to their plays. Sometimes these figures were allegorical – Ate (the goddess of discord) in *Locrine* (*c.* 1590), for example, or Shakespeare's own Rumour. Otherwise, convention seems to have dictated that, cued by the third and final trumpet blast in the open-air playhouses, the role of Chorus was played in a voluminous black cloak and a laurel crown – a suitably 'poetic' surrogate figure for the author himself. Or perhaps not so surrogate if we accept that, like Peter Quince in *A Midsummer Night's Dream*, Shakespeare performed his own Prologues. The disastrous mispunctuation Quince makes of his own words, transforming fawning servility into arrogant indifference (see p. 10), in fact emphasizes the strange mixture of both typically found in the form – as well as the 'quaking' nerves associated with performing it. On the professional stage of the day, a shakily received première could act like a latter-day *New York Times* review and 'sink' an entire production – a nautical metaphor entirely appropriate to London's Bankside theatres.

Shakespeare's use of the device was always experimental. After crafting the Prologue and Act Two Chorus to *Romeo and Juliet* (1594) in the ostentatious form of a sonnet, for example, he seems to have abandoned the framework he envisaged, allowing the mounting tension of the play's action to speak for itself. (It is probably by sheer accident that the second-act Chorus has come down to us at all.) And when he revived and fulfilled that scheme as part of the framework of the six Choruses that punctuate *Henry V* (1599), the effect was to place the heroic action it staged within a sustained set of broadly ironic 'inverted commas', repeatedly and strangely intrusively negotiating the transition from the real to the fictional, from life to art, that is the Prologue's central duty.

Meanwhile, Shakespeare had also brilliantly experimented with a third form of that transition, the device known as the 'Induction'. A sort of theatrical *trompe l'oeil*, the Induction to *The Taming of the Shrew* (1592) introduces the entire play as an entertainment staged for a drunken tinker, Christopher Sly, who is fooled into thinking himself a lord on waking from a night on the town. What is probably an early version of the same play, *The Taming of a Shrew*, elaborates this preamble into a thoroughgoing framework, with Sly at last waking from 'the

4

best dream that ever I had in my life'. Enigmatically, whether by design or accident, no such closure is supplied in the otherwise more authoritative Folio text: as Chuang-Tzu's emperor asked one morning, 'Was I a man dreaming I was a butterfly, or am I a butterfly dreaming I am now a man?' The open-ended dream of the drunken tinker, where lords pretend to be players, and players lords, continues to define the theatrical world Shakespeare helped create.

So to ask a question that Shakespeare himself must so often have pondered, where on earth – or in 'the brightest heaven' – to begin?

'The first and happiest hearers of the town'

These two Prologues, first spoken fourteen years apart, and each introducing a new Shakespeare play, were in all likelihood the first and last examples of the form ever heard at the first Globe theatre, which had opened for business in May 1599, and burned to the ground in June 1613. For all the dazzling effect this sumptuous new 'wooden O' must first have presented, the Chorus to *Henry V* almost grovels for approval in a tone of mock-modesty that simultaneously promotes its audience into 'gentles all', and deprecates even this brand-new playhouse as a mere 'scaffold' (for public executions) or 'cockpit' (for animal-baiting) – instead co-opting their 'imaginary puissance' to the perfection of illusion they will shortly combine to create.

The Prologue to *Henry V* (1599):

CHORUS. O for a muse of fire, that would ascend
    The brightest heaven of invention,
    A kingdom for a stage, princes to act,
    And monarchs to behold the swelling scene!
    Then should the warlike Harry, like himself,
    °Assume the port of Mars; and at his heels,
    Leash'd in like hounds, should famine, sword, and fire

Crouch for employment. But pardon, gentles all,
The °flat unraisèd spirits that have dar'd
On this unworthy scaffold to bring forth
So great an object: can this cockpit hold
The vasty fields of France? Or may we cram
Within this wooden O the very °casques
That did affright the air at Agincourt?
O, pardon! since a crookèd figure may
°Attest in little place a million;
And let us, °ciphers to this great account,
On your imaginary forces work.
Suppose within the girdle of these walls
Are now confin'd two mighty monarchies,
Whose high uprearèd and abutting fronts
The perilous narrow ocean parts asunder.
Piece out our imperfections with your thoughts;
Into a thousand parts divide one man,
And make imaginary puissance.
Think, when we talk of horses, that you see them
Printing their proud hoofs i' th' receiving earth;
For 'tis your thoughts that now must °deck our kings,
Carry them here and there, jumping o'er times,
Turning th'accomplishment of many years
Into an hour-glass: for the which supply,
Admit me Chorus to this history;
Who Prologue-like your humble patience pray,
Gently to hear, kindly to judge, our play.

Fletcher's Chorus to *Henry VIII*, the first in a trio of plays he co-wrote with Shakespeare in the early 1610s, urges the same blend of flattery and friendship upon its 'gentle hearers' – though tastes had changed among the 'first and happiest hearers of the town' at the Globe: no clowns or battle-scenes here – no 'fool and fight' (of the sort *Henry V* had supplied). By an irony of history, the 'wooden O' forever associated with 'a muse of fire' was destroyed 'in two short hours' during a performance of *Henry VIII*, when a stray spark ignited its thatched roof (see pp. 141–3).

John Fletcher, The Prologue to *Henry VIII* (1613):

CHORUS. I come no more to make you laugh: things now
    That bear a weighty and a serious brow,
    Sad, high and working, full of state and woe,
    Such noble scenes as draw the eye to flow,
    We now present. Those that can pity here
    May, if they think it well, let fall a tear;
    The subject will deserve it. Such as give
    Their money out of hope they may believe
    May here find truth, too. Those that come to see
    Only a show or two, and so agree
    The play may pass, if they be still and willing,
    I'll undertake may see away their shilling
    Richly in two short hours. Only they
    That come to hear a merry bawdy play,
    A °noise of targets, or to see a fellow
    In a long °motley coat guarded with yellow,
    Will be deceiv'd. For, gentle hearers, know
    To rank our chosen truth with such a show
    As fool and fight is, beside forfeiting
    Our own brains and the opinion that we bring
    To make that only true we now °intend,
    Will leave us never an understanding friend.
    Therefore, for goodness' sake, and as you are known
    The first and happiest hearers of the town,
    Be sad, as we would make ye; think ye see
    The very persons of our noble story
    As they were living; think you see them great,
    And follow'd with the general throng and sweat
    Of thousand friends; then, in a moment, see
    How soon this mightiness meets misery:
    And, if you can be merry then, I'll say
    A man may weep upon his wedding-day.

'Two hours' traffic'

Shakespeare wrote the Prologue to *Romeo and Juliet* (1594) as a sonnet, swankily flexing his literary muscles as the principal dramatist of the newly founded Lord Chamberlain's Men – one of the two main theatrical 'households' of the day. The promised 'two hours' traffic of our stage' – echoed in Fletcher's 'two short hours' – has been much debated, given the length of many published plays of the time. Whether this reflects a greater rate of delivery on the early modern stage, a piece of conventional rhetoric (like the 'hour-glass' mentioned by *Henry V*'s Chorus), or else (perhaps most likely) that a play's published text routinely supplied more than was ever acted, remains unknown.

The Prologue to *Romeo and Juliet* (1594):

CHORUS. Two households, both alike in dignity,
    In fair Verona, where we lay our scene,
    From ancient grudge break to new mutiny,
    Where civil blood makes civil hands unclean.
    From forth the fatal loins of these two foes
    A pair of star-cross'd lovers take their life,
    Whose misadventur'd piteous overthrows
    Do with their death bury their parents' strife.
    The fearful passage of their death-mark'd love,
    And the continuance of their parents' rage,
    Which °but their children's end nought could remove,
    Is now the two hours' traffic of our stage:
        The which if you with patient ears attend,
        What here shall miss, our toil shall strive to mend.

First-night nerves

Choruses were often written for a specific time and place of performance: a play's court production, for example; or its première on the public stage; or on the occasion of its later revival;

or even in honour of a particular actor's début in a part. They were also therefore among the last pieces of a play's text to be learned, which is perhaps why Shakespeare so often associates the form with 'faintly' spoken hesitation – arguably compounded by his first-hand experience of the 'butterflies' associated with the role. Hence Benvolio's reference below to a 'without-book Prologue'.

Gathered in their costume and masks outside the Capulet ball they are about to gatecrash, Romeo asks his fellow Montagues whether they should deliver the customary oration to their hosts. Benvolio dismisses the idea: such niceties are as antiquated, he says, as the allegorical prologues to old plays – in this case the blindfold figure of Cupid, the boy-god of love, wielding a fearsome-looking bow and arrow, and fumbling over his hastily learned (or half-learned) words. (Interestingly, it is the same figure of Cupid who presents the masque in *Timon of Athens*, the play Shakespeare co-wrote with Thomas Middleton ten years later.) Let them judge ('measure') us instead, says Benvolio, by the quality of our dancing ('measure').

Romeo and Juliet (1594), 1.4:

ROMEO. What, shall this speech be spoke for our excuse?
   Or shall we on, without apology?

BENVOLIO. The date is out of such prolixity:
   We'll have no Cupid, hoodwink'd with a scarf,
   Bearing a Tartar's painted bow of °lath,
   Scaring the ladies like a °crowkeeper;
   Nor no without-book Prologue faintly spoke
   After the prompter, for our entrance.
   But let them measure us by what they will,
   We'll measure them a measure and be gone.

'Certain it is,' wrote Francis Bacon in his treatise on the *Advancement of Learning* (1605), 'that words, as the Tartar's bow, do shoot back upon the understanding of the wisest, and mightily entangle and pervert the judgement.' Whether or not a reference to Benvolio's Cupid, the same boomerang effect is much in evidence in another of Shakespeare's imagined Prologues, this time the nervous recitation by Peter Quince of his own Prologue to *Pyramus and Thisbe* (the play-within-the-play in *A Midsummer Night's Dream*). Unsurprisingly (since the author is delivering his own lines), the speaker is here word-perfect; unfortunately, he is so intent on remembering them, and so stricken by nerves, that the sense of their punctuation ('points') entirely escapes him, and the random pauses and stresses he makes has the devastating effect of reversing its entire meaning. (For the speech as Quince intended it, see below, p. 101.)

A Midsummer Night's Dream (1595), 5.1:

PROLOGUE. 'If we offend, it is with our good will.
　　That you should think. We come not to offend
　　But with good will. To show our simple skill,
　　That is the true beginning of our end.
　　Consider then: we come but in despite.
　　We do not come as minding to content you —
　　Our true intent is. All for your delight
　　We are *not* here: that you should here repent you,
　　The actors are at hand. And by their show
　　You shall know all that you are like to know.'

THESEUS. This fellow doth not stand upon points!

LYSANDER. He hath rid his Prologue like a rough colt: he knows not the stop. A good moral, my lord — it is not enough to speak, but to speak true.

HIPPOLYTA. Indeed, he hath played on this Prologue like a child on a recorder — a sound, but not in government.

THESEUS. His speech was like a tangled chain — nothing impaired, but all disordered.

First-night protection

Audiences are always the ultimate judge of a play's quality, but sometimes the Chorus's traditional 'black velvet cloak and bay garland' required firmer protection. Ben Jonson dressed the Prologue to his *Poetaster* (below) in armour, proof against the attacks for slander his satire on literary London might provoke – disingenuously, since his play, nominally set in Ancient Rome, contains vicious personal assaults on three fellow dramatists (as part of the so-called War of the Theatres). Shakespeare's Chorus to *Troilus and Cressida*, which follows, has sometimes been considered a minor salvo in the same spat. Though likewise arriving 'arm'd' on stage, his Prologue insists on the dramatic propriety of his costume ('In like conditions as our argument') over the potentially self-serving nature of Jonson's style ('but not in confidence / Of author's pen').

from Ben Jonson, The Induction to *Poetaster* (1601):

> *The third sounding.*
>
> *Enter Prologue in armour.*
>
> PROLOGUE. If any °muse why I salute the stage
>   An armèd Prologue, know, 'tis a dangerous age,
>   Wherein who writes had need present his scenes
>   Forty-fold proof against the conjuring means
>   Of base detractors and illiterate apes,
>   That °fill up rooms in fair and formal shapes.
>   'Gainst these have we put on this forc'd defence,
>   Whereof the allegory and hid sense
>   Is that a well-erected confidence
>   Can fright their pride, and laugh their folly hence.

from The Prologue to *Troilus and Cressida* (1601–2):

> CHORUS. Now expectation, tickling skittish spirits
>   On one and other side, Trojan and Greek,
>   Sets all on hazard: and hither am I come
>   A Prologue arm'd, but not in confidence
>   Of author's pen or actor's voice, but suited

In like conditions as our argument,
To tell you, fair beholders, that our play
Leaps o'er the °vaunt and firstlings of those broils,
Beginning in the middle, starting thence away
To what may be digested in a play.
Like or find fault; do as your pleasures are:
Now good or bad, 'tis but the chance of war.

'Think this his barque...'

Perhaps because theatrical architecture held so much technology in common with the Thames-side shipping industry – wooden decking, trap-doors, ropes, ladders, winches, flags, gilding, paintwork, and canvas – the analogy of Chorus to a sort of tug-boat of the imagination must have seemed irresistible. 'In your imagination hold / This stage a ship,' instructs the medieval poet Gower, the Chorus to *Pericles* (one of the riverside Globe's greatest successes), 'upon whose deck / The sea-toss'd Pericles appears to speak.'

from The Fifth and Sixth Choruses of *Pericles* (1608):

GOWER. Thus time we waste and long leagues make short,
　　°Sail seas in cockles, have and wish but for't,
　　Making to take our imagination
　　From °bourn to bourn, region to region.
　　By you being pardon'd, we commit no crime
　　To use one language in each several clime
　　Where our scenes seems to live. I do beseech you
　　To learn of me, who stand i' th' gaps to teach you
　　The stages of our story. Pericles
　　Is now again thwarting the wayward seas [...]
　　So with his steerage shall your thoughts grow on —
　　To fetch his daughter home, who first is gone.
　　Like motes and shadows see them move awhile:
　　Your ears unto your eyes I'll reconcile. [...]
　　In your supposing once more put your sight:
　　Of heavy Pericles, think this his barque,

Where what is done in action — more if might —
Shall be discover'd, please you sit and hark.

While we still speak of the 'launch' of an artistic venture, or the 'pilot' of a television series, recent archaeological evidence demonstrates that timber from broken-up ships was used in the structure of the Rose. The computer consoles and lighting-desks of modern theatres perhaps excuse the apocryphal student who thought the 'cockpit' in the first Chorus to *Henry V* referred to the flight-deck of an aeroplane...

from The Choruses to Acts Two and Three, *Henry V* (1599):

CHORUS. The King is set from London, and the scene
    Is now transported, gentles, to Southampton.
    There is the playhouse now, there must you sit:
    And thence to France shall we convey you safe,
    And bring you back, charming the narrow seas
    To give you gentle pass; for, if we may,
    We'll not offend one stomach with our play.
    But, till the King come forth, and not till then,
    Unto Southampton do we shift our scene. [...]
    Thus with imagin'd wing our swift scene flies
    In motion of no less celerity
    Than that of thought. Suppose that you have seen
    The well-appointed King at Hampton pier
    Embark his royalty, and his brave fleet
    With silken streamers the young °Phoebus fanning.
    Play with your fancies, and in them behold
    Upon the hempen tackle ship-boys climbing;
    Hear the shrill whistle which doth order give
    To sounds confus'd; behold the threaden sails,
    Borne with th'invisible and creeping wind,
    Draw the huge bottoms through the furrow'd sea,
    Breasting the lofty surge.

Co-written with the (in every sense) shady figure of George Wilkins, *Pericles* was based on an old romance by Laurence Twine called *The Pattern of Painful Adventures* (1576, reprinted

1607), a title Wilkins appropriated for his own opportunistic 'novelization' of their vastly successful play, *The Painful Adventures of Pericles, Prince of Tyre* (1608). That word 'adventure' carried overtones of both narrative excitement and commercial endeavour – and therefore supplied the perfect metaphor for Shakespeare's entrepreneurial career in the marketplace of his theatre. A generation later, the playwright Henry Glapthorne elegantly summarized the conceit in a Prologue he composed for a young actor graduating for the first time from female roles (while also demonstrating the 'one-off' status such speeches so often embodied).

from Henry Glapthorne, 'Prologue for Ezekiel Fenn at his First Acting a Man's Part' (1639):

PROLOGUE. Suppose a merchant when he launches forth
   An untried vessel, doubtful of its worth,
   Dare not adventure on that infant piece
   The glorious fetching of a °Golden Fleece
   From the remot'st Indies: 'tis so with me,
   Whose innocence and timorous modesty
   Does blush at my own shadow, prone to fear
   Each wave a billow that arises here.
   The company's my merchant, nor dare they
   Expose my weak frame on so rough a sea
   'Less you (their skilful pilots) please to steer
   By mild direction of your eye and ear
   Their new-rigg'd barque.

'Passionate action'

The convention of a play's mimed plot-summary or allegorical commentary, performed over music (the Elizabethan equivalent, perhaps, of a Wagnerian overture), was already old-hat by the time Shakespeare began writing for the professional stage in the early 1590s, though the Dumb Show continued to provide a useful shorthand to signal a 'play-within-the-play' (in

Hamlet and *A Midsummer Night's Dream*, for example). The device overlapped with, and was eventually superseded by, the figure of the Presenter, or Prologue, who explained the 'argument'. As Gower promises in the Third Chorus to *Pericles*, 'What's dumb in show I'll plain [= *clarify*] with speech.' Ben Jonson had meanwhile wittily distinguished between the two forms in an elaborate metaphor of the ways in which love-lorn men can behave. So while one such suitor nervously rehearses his chat-up lines in the moments before meeting his beloved, and 'repeats, / Like an unperfect Prologue at third music, / His part of speeches... In passion to himself', another is so paralysed by nerves that he 'only comes in for a Mute, / Divides the Act with a Dumb Show, and *Exit*' (*Cynthia's Revels* (1600), 3.2).

Shakespeare lays on quite a series of overtures to *The Murder of Gonzago* (alias *The Mousetrap*), the play-within-the-play in *Hamlet*, perhaps in compensation for its later abrupt abandonment. We have the fanfare familiar from the public theatres ('*The trumpets sound*' – interestingly moved indoors by the later Folio text, which substitutes '*Hautboys play*'), followed by the elaborate Dumb Show itself (which in the 1603 First Quarto text specifies that the murderer enters 'with poison in a vial'). The 'argument of the play' to which Ophelia refers may relate to the formal synopsis of a play's action that was distributed – much like a modern opera programme – among richer audiences in the period ('Have you heard the argument?' asks Claudius later. 'Is there no offence in't?'). *Hamlet*'s first audiences must in any case have wondered what they were in for – especially since *Hamlet* itself had bypassed the process entirely with its stark opening on the battlements of Elsinore ('Who's there?'). *The Mousetrap*'s Prologue prolongs the tension; its redundant brevity clinches the suspense.

Hamlet (1600–1; Q2 1604–5), 3.2:

> *The trumpets sounds. Dumb Show follows.*
>
> *Enter a* KING *and* QUEEN, *the* QUEEN *embracing him, and he her. He takes her up and declines his head upon her neck. He lies him down upon a bank of flowers. She seeing him*

asleep leaves him. Anon come in another MAN, *takes off his crown, kisses it, pours poison in the sleeper's ears, and leaves him. The* QUEEN *returns, finds the* KING *dead, makes passionate action. The* POISONER *with some three or four come in again, seem to condole with her. The dead body is carried away. The* POISONER *woos the* QUEEN *with gifts. She seems harsh awhile but in the end accepts love.*

Exeunt.

OPHELIA. What means this, my lord?

HAMLET. Marry, this °miching mallico? It means mischief.

OPHELIA. Belike this show imports the argument of the play.

Enter PROLOGUE.

HAMLET. We shall know by this fellow. The players cannot keep counsel: they'll tell all.

OPHELIA. Will he tell us what this show meant?

HAMLET. Ay, or any show that you will show him. Be not you ashamed to show, he'll not shame to tell you what it means.

OPHELIA. You are °naught, you are naught. I'll mark the play.

PROLOGUE. 'For us, and for our tragedy,
       Here stooping to your clemency,
       We beg your hearing patiently.'

Exit.

HAMLET. Is this a prologue or the °posy of a ring?

OPHELIA. 'Tis brief, my lord.

HAMLET. As woman's love.

Breaking the fourth wall

In Shakespeare's theatre, one habitually spoke of going to 'hear' rather than 'see' a play. Nevertheless, that theatre presented the ideal opportunity for a certain class of spectator both to see and be seen – whether in the 'Lords' rooms' at the public open-air playhouses, or in the case of the private indoor theatre at Blackfriars, on the stage itself, upstage of the playing-space, in constant and prominent view. Thomas Dekker sarcastically advised boorish gentlemen on the etiquette of disrupting a play's opening most effectively by arriving, as we would say, 'fashionably late', silver coin ('teston') in hand to tip the usher.

from Thomas Dekker, °*The Gull's Hornbook* (1609):

> Present not yourself on the stage (especially at a new play) until the quaking Prologue hath by rubbing got colour into his cheeks, and is ready to give the trumpets their cue that he's upon point to enter; for then it is time, as though you were one of the properties, or that you dropped out of the hangings, to creep from behind the arras, with your tripos (or three-footed stool) in one hand, and a teston mounted between a forefinger and a thumb in the other. For if you should bestow your person upon the vulgar when the belly of the house is but half full, your apparel is quite eaten up, the fashion lost.

The relative impossibility of naturalistic illusion under such conditions prompted two distinct strategies among playwrights. The first, as we have seen above, was the repeated co-opting of an audience's imagination by the plays' Prologues and Choruses. The second was to deliberately blur the unignorable distinction between audience and actors by constructing a further layer somewhere in between – a framing narrative, in other words, that dissolved the so-called 'fourth wall' by casting members of the company as audience-members, backstage theatre staff, or even… members of the company themselves.

Shakespeare seems to have been drawn to such 'meta-theatrical' tricks from the first, inadvertently bequeathing an endless textual headache to future scholars in the form of the two surviving versions of what is probably his earliest play. *The Taming of the Shrew* was first published in the 1623 First Folio, nearly thirty years after *The Taming of a Shrew* had appeared in a Quarto edition (1594) – and that is about all we know for certain about how these two plays relate to one another. Both plays erect their essentially identical action about a framework in which a dissolute vagabond called Christopher Sly is fooled into believing himself an amnesiac lord on waking from a drunken stupor. The illusion is sustained by a company of touring players on a visit to a *real* lord, who contrives to have one of his page-boys impersonate the nonplussed Sly's wife, instructing the actors to perform their play for their benefit. One recent editor of *The Taming of the Shrew* playfully divides its Dramatis Personae between those who feature in the play's 'Induction' (Christopher Sly *et al.*), and those appearing in its 'Play-within-the-Play' (including Kate and Petruchio) – which prompts the question as to where 'the play' itself, in its two variant states, ultimately resides.

from The Induction to *The Taming of a Shrew* (1590):

Enter a MESSENGER.

MESSENGER. °An it please your honour, your players be come,
And do attend your honour's pleasure here.

LORD. The fittest time they could have chosen out!
Bid one or two of them come hither straight.

Exit MESSENGER.

Now will I fit myself accordingly,
For they shall play to him when he awakes.

Enter two of the PLAYERS, *with packs at their backs, and a* BOY.

Now, sirs, what store of plays have you?

1 PLAYER. Marry, my lord, you may have a Tragical or a
Commodity, or what you will.

2 PLAYER (*aside to him*). A 'Comedy' thou shouldst say —
zounds, thou'lt shame us all!

LORD. And what's the name of your Comedy?

1 PLAYER. Marry, my lord, 'tis called *The Taming of a Shrew*.
'Tis a good lesson for us, my lord — for us that are
married men.

LORD. *The Taming of a Shrew*? That's excellent, sure.
Go see that you make you ready straight,
For you must play before a lord tonight.
Say you are his men, and I your fellow.

Ben Jonson went on to play a similar game with frames in
the Induction ('not for want of a Prologue, but by way of a
new one') to his sprawling masterpiece of London life,
Bartholomew Fair. It is one thing to view a fiction in which a
set of obviously fictional characters prepare to perform a play
we are about to watch ('*The Taming of a Shrew*? That's excellent, sure'); it was something complicatedly different,
though, to find oneself in the audience of a new play at the
Hope theatre, being directly addressed by (the actors playing) the theatre's prompter ('book-holder') and copyist
('scrivener'). Shakespeare's Choruses insist on the mutual
imaginative endeavour that an audience and company could
co-create; Jonson spells out the humbler transactions
involved whenever 'market forces' seek to place 'bums on
seats'.

from Ben Jonson, 'The Induction on the Stage',
Bartholomew Fair (1614)

BOOK-HOLDER. Gentlemen, not for want of a Prologue, but
by way of a new one, I am sent out to you here, with
a scrivener, and certain articles drawn out in haste
between our author and you; which if you please to
hear, and as they appear reasonable, to approve of,
the play will follow presently. — Read, scribe, gi' me
the °counterpane.

SCRIVENER. 'Articles of agreement, indented, between the spectators, or hearers, at the Hope on the Bankside, in the county of Surrey on the one party , and the author of *Bartholomew Fair* in the said place and county on the other party: the one-and-thirtieth day of October 1614, and in the twelfth year of the reign of our Sovereign Lord James, by the grace of God King of England, France, and Ireland, Defender of the Faith, and of Scotland the seven-and-fortieth:

'IMPRIMIS, it is covenanted and agreed, by and between the parties abovesaid, that the said spectators and hearers, as well the curious and envious as the favouring and judicious, as also the °grounded judgements and understandings, do for themselves severally covenant and agree to remain in the places their money or friends have put them in, with patience, for the space of two hours and a half, and somewhat more. In which time the author promiseth to present them, by us, with a new sufficient play called *Bartholomew Fair*, merry, and as full of noise as sport, made to delight all, and to offend none — provided they have either the wit or the honesty to think well of themselves.'

Shakespeare always associated music with healing; perhaps he felt the same way about drama ('Doctor Theatre', as the saying still goes). And so in what is perhaps his earliest play, a Servant (played by a Lord) introduces that play to a Beggar (who imagines himself a Lord) and to his wife (played by a Servant), in hopes of easing the alcoholic depression that afflicts him. And that (at least in the Folio text) is the last we ever hear of them. Whoever these characters really are, and however we 'frame' how we see them, their 'pleasant comedy' somehow 'lengthens life' – and even if it doesn't, 'We shall ne'er be younger', and we might as well enjoy ourselves along the way.

from The Induction to *The Taming of the Shrew* (1592), Scene 2:

SERVANT. Your honour's players, hearing your amendment,
　　Are come to play a pleasant comedy;
　　For so your doctors hold it very meet,
　　Seeing too much sadness hath congeal'd your blood,
　　And melancholy is the nurse of frenzy:
　　Therefore they thought it good you hear a play
　　And frame your mind to mirth and merriment,
　　Which bars a thousand harms and lengthens life.

SLY. Marry, I will. Let them play it. Is not a °commonty a
　　Christmas gambol or a tumbling-trick?

PAGE. No, my good lord, it is more pleasing stuff.

SLY. What, household stuff?

PAGE. 　　　　　　　　　　It is a kind of history.

SLY. Well, we'll see't. Come, Madam Wife, sit by my side,
　　and let the world slip. We shall ne'er be younger.

In 1604, the King's Men – Shakespeare's newly promoted company – gained possession of the theatre copy (or 'book') of John Marston's recent hit play *The Malcontent*. The play had enjoyed great success in the repertoire of a company of boy actors, the Children of the Chapel Royal. For complicated reasons, however, the play transferred from the exclusive Blackfriars theatre (where it was performed indoors in the evening) to the daylight stage of the public Globe – and the company commissioned a new and elaborate 'Induction' for the occasion from the up-and-coming dramatist John Webster. The new scene playfully imagines a well-dressed 'gallant', a fan of the play, emerging from the waiting crowd to claim a place on the stage, to view it at close quarters, as was his right at the Blackfriars – but not at the Globe. After an argument with the dresser ('tire-man'), he demands to speak to three of the company's best-known actors, but although Burbage, Condell, and Lowin then enter 'as themselves', Will Sly remains backstage – or rather he doesn't, since it is Will Sly who is playing the gallant in the first place. Webster's casting, in this dazzling hall of theatrical mirrors, may owe something to Will Sly's namesake Christopher in *The Taming of the Shrew*, a role the actor may also have performed. Meanwhile Shakespeare himself seems to have been waiting in the wings, as ever just out of sight.

John Webster, Induction (1604) to *The Malcontent* (1603) by John Marston:

> *Enter* WILL SLY *as a gallant playgoer, a* TIRE-MAN *following him with a stool, on to the stage of the Globe.*

TIRE-MAN. Sir, the gentlemen will be angry if you sit here.

SLY. Why? We may sit upon the stage at the private house. Thou dost not take me for a country gentleman, dost? Dost think I fear hissing? I'll hold my life thou took'st me for one of the players!

TIRE-MAN. No, sir!

SLY. By °God's-lid, if you had, I would have given you but sixpence for your stool. (*Sits.*) Let them that have stale suits sit in the galleries. Hiss at me? He that will be laughed out of a tavern or an °ordinary shall seldom feed well or be drunk in good company. Where's Harry Condell, Dick Burbage, and Will Sly? Let me speak with some of them.

TIRE-MAN. An't please you to go in, sir, you may.

SLY. I tell you no. I am one that hath seen this play often, and can give them intelligence for their action. I have most of the jests here in my table-book.

> *Enter* JOHN SINCKLO *as* SLY's *gentleman relative.*

SINCKLO. Save you, coz.

SLY. O cousin, come — you shall sit between my legs here.

SINCKLO. No indeed, cousin. The audience then will take me for a °viol da gamba, and think that you play upon me.

SLY. Nay, rather that I work upon you, coz.

SINCKLO. We °stayed for you at supper last night. [...]

Enter DICK BURBAGE, HARRY CONDELL, *and* JOHN LOWIN *as themselves.*

What be these, coz?

SLY. The players. (*Stands, removes his hat, and bows.*) God save you!

BURBAGE. You are very welcome. [...]

SLY. I would know how you came by this play.

CONDELL. Faith, sir, the book was lost, and because 'twas pity so good a play should be lost, we found it and play it.

SLY. I wonder you would play it, another company having interest in it.

CONDELL. Why not °Malevole in Folio with us, as Jeronimo in Decimo-Sexto with them? They taught us a name for our play: we call it *One for Another.*

SLY. What are your additions?

BURBAGE. Sooth, not greatly needful — only as your salad to your great feast: to entertain a little more time, and to abridge the not-received custom of music in our theatre. I must leave you, sir.

Exit BURBAGE.

SINCKLO. Doth he play the Malcontent?

CONDELL. Yes, sir. [...]

LOWIN (*to* SLY). Good sir, will you leave the stage? I'll help you to a private room.

SLY. Come, coz, let's take some tobacco. — Have you never a Prologue?

LOWIN. Not any, sir.

SLY. Let me see: I will make one extempore. Come to them and, fencing of a °congée with arms and legs, be round with them:

(*To the audience.*) 'Gentlemen, I could wish for the women's sakes you all had soft cushions. And gentlewomen, I could wish that for the men's sakes you had all more °easy standings.' (*To* LOWIN.) What would they wish more but the play now? — and that they shall have instantly.

Exeunt.

As Webster's Induction to *The Malcontent* demonstrates, playgoers at the turn of the seventeenth century were becoming increasingly sophisticated devotees of the backstage gossip and literary rivalries of an embryonic celebrity culture, an interest indulged by the variety of Prologues and Inductions the dramatists supplied. Perhaps the closest Shakespeare ever came to any such direct commentary is the conversation in *Hamlet* between the Prince and his student friends, when a touring troupe of players arrives at Elsinore. The rivalry Rosencrantz reports, between the established adult actors and the newly successful children's companies, has long been recognized as an oblique commentary on the so-called War of the Theatres ('there has been much to-do on both sides') – which is perhaps why most of the sequence was omitted as old news from the play's otherwise authoritative Second Quarto (1604–5), and not published until the 1623 Folio. As Guildenstern summarizes the gist in the play's First Quarto (1603), 'the principal public audience that came to them are turned to private plays, and to the humour of children'. The famous description of the Children of the Chapel Royal as a nest of fledgling falcons ('an eyrie of children, litle eyases') forms part of an extended series of references to birds throughout the play, from the 'bird of dawning' that shoos away the Ghost in its first scene, to Hamlet's acknowledgement in its last that 'There is special providence in the fall of a sparrow'.

Hamlet (1600–1), 2.2:

HAMLET. What players are they?

ROSENCRANTZ. Even those you were wont to take such delight in: the tragedians of the city.

HAMLET. How chances it they travel? Their residence, both in reputation and profit, was better both ways.

ROSENCRANTZ. I think their inhibition comes by the means of the °late innovation.

HAMLET. Do they hold the same estimation they did when I was in the city? Are they so followed?

ROSENCRANTZ. No, indeed are they not.

HAMLET. How comes it? Do they grow rusty?

ROSENCRANTZ. Nay, their endeavour keeps in the wonted pace; but there is, sir, an eyrie of children, little eyases, that cry out on the top of question, and are most tyrannically clapped for it. These are now the fashion and so berattle the common stages — so they call them — that many wearing rapiers are afraid of goose-quills and dare scarce come thither.

HAMLET. What, are they children? Who maintains 'em? How are they °escoted? Will they pursue the quality no longer than they can sing? Will they not say afterwards, if they should grow themselves to common players (as it is most like, if their means are no better), their writers do them wrong to make them exclaim against their own succession?

ROSENCRANTZ. Faith, there has been much to-do on both sides; and the nation holds it no sin to °tar them to controversy. There was for a while no money bid for argument unless the poet and the player went to °cuffs in the question.

HAMLET. Is't possible?

GUILDENSTERN. O, there has been much throwing about of brains.

HAMLET. Do the boys carry it?

ROSENCRANTZ. Ay, that they do, my lord — Hercules and his load, too.

On the face of it, Rosencrantz tells Hamlet that the success of these upstart companies (as the expression still has it) carries the world before them. In the immediate context of the play's first performances, however, the reference to Hercules' temporary shouldering of the weight of the world – or Globe – will have been unmistakable.

The supposed motto of the Globe theatre (1599):

Totus mundus agit histrionem.

('Everyone in the world is playing a role'; alternative translation: 'All the world's a stage.')

1
Auditions, Casting, and Parts

Their various characters they choose with art:
The frowning bully fits the tyrant's part;
Swoll'n cheeks and swaggering belly make an host,
Pale meagre looks and hollow voice a ghost;
From careful brows and heavy downcast eyes
Dull °cits and thick-skull'd aldermen arise [...]
Thus several persons several parts perform:
Soft lovers whine, and blustering heroes storm;
The stern exasperated tyrants rage,
Till the kind bowl of poison clears the stage.

Joseph Addison (c. 1700)

The world is a stage, but the play is badly cast.

Oscar Wilde (1891)

However Shakespeare managed his obscure elopement to
the theatre in the late 1580s, he had already raised eye-
brows among his peers as an 'upstart crow' by the time his
name featured as a principal member of the Lord Chamberlain's Men in 1594, alongside those of its leading actor Richard
Burbage and celebrated clown Will Kemp. The opportunities
presented by a permanent theatrical company, around fifteen-
strong, and (after 1599) by a custom-built playhouse,
increasingly absorbed Shakespeare's capacious imagination.
Within a year of the Lord Chamberlain's Men's first group
rehearsals, he was fondly mocking the whole business of amateur theatricals in *A Midsummer Night's Dream* (1595), casting

Kemp as the bumptious wannabe Nick Bottom and (a likely conjecture) himself as the exasperated author–director Peter Quince. Within five years of their foundation, they were installed at the Globe, producing spectacular new plays whose *dramatis personae* ran into dozens of carefully doubled parts. Within a decade, company-members were famous enough to be impersonated by precocious university undergraduates – as well as by the actors themselves at the Globe, as we have seen.

We know something of Shakespeare's casting-decisions from the residual evidence of his published plays – and not simply from such obvious deductions as that Kemp the clown played the roles so frequently assigned to 'Clown' in his stage-directions. He also seems to have noted those decisions in short-hand as he wrote. In Act Four of the earliest texts of *Much Ado About Nothing* (1598), for example, the parts of Dogberry and Verges are assigned to 'Kemp' and 'Cowley'; and when the parish constable arrives to arrest Doll Tearsheet in *Henry IV, Part Two* (1598), it is 'Sincklo' who enters the play's 1600 Quarto. The names 'William Kempt' and 'Richard Cowly' appear in the 1623 Folio's list of 'the Principal Actors in all these Plays', while the skinny John Sincklo seems to have given a series of lugubrious cameos, from the Apothecary in *Romeo and Juliet* (1594) to, as we've seen, Sly's diminutive cousin in Webster's Induction to *The Malcontent* (1604).

The artistic security, professional resources, and increasing wealth of the Lord Chamberlain's Men – promoted to King's Men in 1603 – immeasurably facilitated Shakespeare's work, enabling him to tailor his parts to the proven skills of his colleagues' accomplished turns. 'Tailoring the parts' is no idle metaphor, since the finished scripts he delivered were routinely transcribed and distributed among the company as individual 'part-scripts', each marked up with the preceding cues and requisite stage-directions (hence their alternative designation as 'parts in cue' or 'cue-scripts'), before being each stitched together to form a paper roll, or scroll – the 'role' by which (via the French) theatrical parts have come to be known.

In an age when most men inherited their occupation, lifestyle, and status from their fathers and forefathers, and when almost all women were constrained to the submissive demands of their biology, the very *idea* of multiple impersonation – the sheer notion that any single individual might play more than the single part society had prescribed them – remained a fascinating and thrilling one. No wonder the lowly Athenian weaver Nick Bottom – or come to that, the lowly Stratford apprentice-glover Will Shakespeare – so yearned to play *all* the parts that came his way. And so, in a sense, they both did. Like the enigmatically open-ended dream of Christopher Sly, Shakespeare's imagination ranged across the conventional 'estates' of medieval hierarchy, from King to Clown, via Knight and Knave, and his characters repeatedly contemplate – and frequently exchange – the roles they find themselves playing. 'To prove his best, and if none here gainsay it,' as Heywood's later Prologue to Marlowe's *Jew of Malta* puts it (1633), 'The part he hath studied, and intends to play it'. For men of Heywood's – and Shakespeare's – generation, that promise was as much a social declaration as a professional appeal.

'Is all our company here?'

It is revealing of Shakespeare's mind and inspiration that his Prince of Denmark shares the humble weaver Nick Bottom's passion for the theatre. Bottom aspires to a starring role (or three) in an amateur production, while Hamlet – having delivered an impromptu audition piece to the Players, and caught the 'conscience of the King' in their play – jests *de haut en bas* about the credentials required to wear the feathered costumes and fashionable shoes of a professional company. It is surely no accident that both these backstage glimpses concern the 'fellowship' and 'company' of old friends.

A Midsummer Night's Dream (1595), 1.2:

QUINCE. Is all our company here?

BOTTOM. You were best to call them generally, man by man, according to the °scrip.

QUINCE. Here is the scroll of every man's name which is thought fit through all Athens to play in our Interlude before the Duke and the Duchess on his wedding-day at night.

BOTTOM. First, good Peter Quince, say what the play treats on; then read the names of the actors; and so °grow to a point.

QUINCE. Marry, our play is *The Most Lamentable Comedy and Most Cruel Death of Pyramus and Thisbe.*

BOTTOM. A very good piece of work, I assure you, and a merry. Now, good Peter Quince, call forth your actors by the scroll. Masters, spread yourselves.

QUINCE. Answer as I call you. Nick Bottom the weaver!

BOTTOM. Ready! Name what part I am for, and proceed.

QUINCE. You, Nick Bottom, are set down for Pyramus.

BOTTOM. What is Pyramus? A Lover or a Tyrant?

QUINCE. A Lover, that kills himself most gallantly for love.

BOTTOM. That will ask some tears in the true performing of it. If I do it, let the audience look to their eyes: I will move storms; I will °condole in some measure. To the rest. — Yet, my chief humour is for a Tyrant. I could play °Ercles rarely, or a part to tear a cat in, to make all split —

> 'The raging rocks
> And shivering shocks
> Shall break the locks
>   Of prison gates,
> And °Phibbus' car
> Shall shine from far,
> And make and mar
>   The foolish Fates.'

This was lofty. Now name the rest of the players. — This is Ercles' vein, a Tyrant's vein; a Lover is more condoling.

QUINCE. Francis Flute, the bellows-mender!

FLUTE. Here, Peter Quince.

QUINCE. You must take Thisbe on you.

FLUTE. What is Thisbe? A wand'ring Knight?

QUINCE. It is the lady that Pyramus must love.

FLUTE. Nay, faith, let not me play a woman — I have a
beard coming.

QUINCE. That's all one, you shall play it in a mask, and
you may speak as small as you will.

BOTTOM. °An I may hide my face, let me play Thisbe too!
I'll speak in a monstrous little voice — 'Thisne,
Thisne!' — 'Ah, Pyramus, my lover dear, thy Thisbe
dear, and lady dear —'

QUINCE. No, no, you must play Pyramus — and Flute,
you Thisbe.

BOTTOM. Well, proceed.

QUINCE. Robin Starveling, the tailor!

STARVELING. Here, Peter Quince.

QUINCE. Robin Starveling, you must play Thisbe's
mother. — Tom Snout, the tinker!

SNOUT. Here, Peter Quince.

QUINCE. You, Pyramus' father; myself, Thisbe's father;
Snug the joiner, you the lion's part. And I hope there is
a play °fitted.

Hamlet (1600–1), 3.2:

HAMLET. Would not this, sir, and a forest of feathers — if
the rest of my fortunes turn Turk with me — with
°provincial roses on my razed shoes, get me a
°fellowship in a cry of players?

HORATIO. Half a share.

HAMLET. A whole one, I —

31

'For thou dost know, O °Damon dear,
  This realm dismantlèd was
Of Jove himself, and now reigns here,
  A very, very — °pajock.'

HORATIO. You might have rhymed.

Contemporary opinion recommended two main alternatives for a successful actor: either that the candidate be intelligent enough to understand the argument of his speech, and therefore be able to convey the sense of its subtleties; or else, gifted with a powerful and expressive voice, surmount his limited understanding of the script by the sheer charisma of his stage presence. (The same alternative credentials arguably pertain to this day.) Ideally, of course, both qualities were required – whether in the 'good tongue' and 'good conceit' recommended by Shakespeare's junior contemporary Thomas Heywood, or the 'good accent and good discretion' Polonius praises in the stagestruck Hamlet's impromptu recital from memory at what starts as the Players' audition.

from Thomas Heywood, *An Apology for Actors* (1612):

> Actors should be men picked out personable, according to the parts they present. They should be rather scholars, that though they cannot speak well, know how to speak, or else to have that volubility that they can speak well, though they understand not what, and so both imperfections may by instructions be helped and amended. But where a good tongue and a good conceit both fail, there can never be good actor.

Hamlet (1600–1), 2.2:

Enter the PLAYERS.

HAMLET. You are welcome, masters; welcome, all. — I am
  glad to see thee well. — Welcome, good friends. — O,
  my old friend! Thy face is °valanced since I saw thee
  last: com'st thou to beard me in Denmark? — What,

my young lady and mistress! By'r lady, your ladyship is
nearer to heaven than when I saw you last, by the
°altitude of a chopine. Pray God your voice, like a piece
of uncurrent gold, be not °cracked within the ring. —
Masters, you are all welcome. We'll e'en to't like
French falconers: fly at anything we see. We'll have a
speech straight. Come, give us a taste of your quality;
come, a passionate speech.

1 PLAYER. What speech, my good lord?

HAMLET. I heard thee speak me a speech once, but it was
never acted; or, if it was, not above once; for the play, I
remember, pleased not the million; 'twas °caviare to
the general: but it was (as I received it, and others,
whose judgements in such matters °cried in the top of
mine) an excellent play, well digested in the scenes, set
down with as much °modesty as cunning. I remember,
one said there were no °sallets in the lines to make the
matter savoury, nor no matter in the phrase that might
indict the author of affectation; but called it an honest
method, as wholesome as sweet, and by very much
more handsome than fine. One speech in it I chiefly
loved: 'twas °Aeneas' tale to Dido; and thereabout of it
especially where he speaks of °Priam's slaughter. If it
live in your memory, begin at this line — let me see, let
me see —

'The ruggèd °Pyrrhus, like th'°Hyrcanian beast—'

It is not so — it begins with Pyrrhus.

'The ruggèd Pyrrhus (he whose °sable arms,
Black as his purpose, did the night resemble
When he lay couchèd in the ominous horse)
Hath now this dread and black complexion smear'd
With heraldry more dismal. Head to foot
Now is he total gules, horridly trick'd
With blood of fathers, mothers, daughters, sons,
Bak'd and impasted with the parching streets
That lend a tyrannous and damnèd light
To their lord's murder. Roasted in wrath and fire,

And thus °o'er-sizèd with coagulate gore,
With eyes like °carbuncles, the hellish Pyrrhus
Old grandsire Priam seeks…'

So, proceed you.

POLONIUS. 'Fore God, my lord, well spoken, with good
accent and good discretion.

Of course, very few auditions ever result in a perfect cast, especially in amateur productions, with their limited resources, as
the pedantic scholar Holofernes is forced to recognize when
planning his pageant of the Nine Worthies (or exemplary
heroes). Running out of actors to cast all nine, he selflessly vol-
unteers to play three of them himself. (The page-boy Moth
offers some usefully playful advice on how to convert a heckle
into applause.)

Love's Labour's Lost (1595), 5.1:

HOLOFERNES. Sir Nathaniel, as concerning some
entertainment of time, some show in the posterior of
this day, to be rendered by our assistance, the King's
command, and this most gallant, illustrate, and learned
gentleman, before the Princess — I say, none so fit as
to present 'The Nine Worthies'.

NATHANIEL. Where will you find men worthy enough to
present them?

HOLOFERNES. Joshua, yourself; this gallant gentleman,
Judas Maccabeus; this swain, because of his great limb
or joint, shall pass Pompey the Great; the page,
Hercules—

ARMADO. Pardon, sir, error! He is not quantity enough
for that Worthy's thumb — he is not so big as the end
of his club.

HOLOFERNES. Shall I °have audience? He shall present
°Hercules in minority: his enter and exit shall be
strangling a snake; and I will have an °apology for that
purpose.

MOTH. An excellent device! So if any of the audience hiss, you may cry, 'Well done, Hercules! Now thou crushest the snake!' That is the way to make an offence gracious, though few have the grace to do it.

ARMADO. For the rest of the Worthies?

HOLOFERNES. I will play three myself.

MOTH. Thrice-worthy gentleman!

Town vs. gown

Shakespeare's poetic facility had raised hackles and ruffled feathers among the 'University Wits' – those Oxbridge play-wrights upon whose intellectual preserve he was accused of trespassing. The playwright and pamphleteer Robert Greene (MA Cantab, MA Oxon) – or someone purporting to be him, probably Henry Chettle – described the Swan of Avon as an 'upstart crow', and perverted one of Shakespeare's own lines ('O tiger's heart wrapp'd in a woman's hide!' from *Henry VI, Part Three*) to express his disdain.

from Greene's *Groatsworth of Wit* (1592):

> Yes, trust them not: for there is an upstart crow, beautified with our feathers, that with his *Tiger's heart wrapp'd in a Player's hide* supposes he is as well able to bombast out a blank verse as the best of you: and being an absolute °*Johannes factotum* is in his own conceit the only Shake-scene in the country.

Shakespeare attended neither Oxford nor Cambridge, which might lend a tang to Hamlet's interrupted education at Wit-tenberg, and his guying of the elderly alumnus Polonius. His influence, however, was felt in both. When the first edition of *Hamlet* was published in 1603, its title-page blurb celebrated its many performances in London, 'as also in the two Universi-ties' – where the company seem to have gained a student fan-base. Or so the 1601–2 Christmas play at St John's, Cambridge, seems to indicate, featuring as it does an impromptu audition of two undergraduates by none other than Burbage and Kemp themselves.

Hamlet (1601–2), 3.2:

HAMLET. You played once i' th'University, you say?

POLONIUS. That did I, my lord, and was accounted a good actor.

HAMLET. What did you enact?

POLONIUS. I did enact Julius Caesar. I was killed i' th' Capitol. Brutus killed me.

HAMLET. It was a °brute part of him to kill so capital a calf there. — Be the players ready?

The characterization of Burbage and Kemp by the anonymous Cambridge playwright quoted below reflects a close interest in contemporary theatrical practice – and gossip. Kemp observes, for example, that amateur performers tend to enter the stage, then artificially walk all the way to the front of it in silence, before beginning to deliver their lines; unlike at the Globe, presumably, where the dialogue was essentially continuous, and therefore more realistic. News has also reached Cambridge of the recent 'War of the Theatres' in London (though quite how Shakespeare has managed to best Ben Jonson and 'beray his credit', or *defile his reputation*, remains endlessly debated), and of Kemp's recent return from a continental tour of Germany and Italy. The author's blend of affectionate admiration for Kemp, intellectual condescension towards him ('that writer Metamorphoses'),* and palpable envy of his fame, is one that feels familiar to this day in the often spiky relationship between the Academy and the Theatre. The audition pieces Burbage goes on to suggest are (rather cruelly) two of his greatest triumphs: soliloquies by the

---

* In fact of course the title of Ovid's most famous work, and Shakespeare's obvious favourite.

revenger-hero Hieronymo in *The Spanish Tragedy* by Thomas Kyd, and Shakespeare's Richard III.

Anon., *The Second Part of the Return from Parnassus* (1601–2), 4.3–4.4:

BURBAGE. Now, Will Kemp, if we can °entertain these scholars at a low rate, it will be well. They have oftentimes a good conceit in a part.

KEMP. It's true indeed, honest Dick, but the slaves are somewhat proud. And besides, 'tis good sport in a part to see them never speak in their walk but at the end of the stage, just as though in walking with a fellow we should never speak but at a stile, a gate, or a ditch, where a man can go no further. I was once at a comedy in Cambridge, and there I saw a parasite make faces and mouths of all sorts on this fashion.

BURBAGE. A little teaching will mend these faults, and it may be besides they will be able to pen a part.

KEMP. Few of the University pen plays well. They smell too much of that writer Ovid, and that writer Metamorphoses, and talk too much of Proserpina and Jupiter. Why, here's our fellow Shakespeare puts them all down — ay, and Ben Jonson too. O, that Ben Jonson is a pestilent fellow — he brought up Horace giving the poets a pill, but our fellow Shakespeare hath given him a purge that made him beray his credit.

BURBAGE. It's a shrewd fellow indeed. I wonder these scholars stay so long. They appointed to be here presently that we might try them. Oh, here they come —

Enter PHILOMUSUS *and* STUDIOSO. […]

God save you. […]

PHILOMUSUS. The same to you, good Master Burbage. What, Master Kemp, how doth the Emperor of Germany?

STUDIOSO. God save you, Master Kemp. Welcome, Master Kemp, from dancing the morris over the Alps.

KEMP. Well, you merry knaves, you may come to the honour of it one day. Is't not better to make a fool of the world, as I have done, than to be fooled of the world, as you scholars are? But be merry, my lads, you have happened upon the most excellent vocation in the world! For money, they come north and south to bring it to our playhouse; and for honour, who of more report than Dick Burbage and Will Kemp? He's not counted a gentleman that knows not Dick Burbage and Will Kemp. [...]

BURBAGE. Master Studioso, I pray you take some part in this book, and act it, that I may see what will fit you best. I think your voice would serve for Hieronymo. Observe how I act it, and then imitate me.

'Who calls Hieronymo from his naked bed?'

STUDIOSO. 'Who calls Hieronymo from his naked bed?' &c.

BURBAGE. You will do well after a while.

KEMP. Now for you. Methinks you should belong to my tuition, and your face methinks would be good for a foolish Mayor, or a foolish Justice of Peace. [...]

BURBAGE. I like your face and the proportion of your body for Richard the Third. I pray you, Master Philomusus, let me see you act a little of it.

PHILOMUSUS. 'Now is the winter of our discontent
Made glorious summer by the son of York,' &c.

BURBAGE. Very well, I assure you. Well, Master Philomusus and Master Studioso, we see what ability you are of. I pray walk with us to our fellows, and we'll °agree presently. [...]

Exeunt BURBAGE *and* KEMP.

PHILOMUSUS. And must the basest trade yield us relief?
Must we be practis'd to those leaden spouts
That nought do °vent but what they do receive?

'He that plays the King…'

Whether or not he performed his own Choruses, Shakespeare seems to have largely cast himself in what we would call 'character parts', and in any case maintained a thorough understanding of his actors' range – as the following extracts reveal. 'Old Men' were a speciality of his own – traditionally including 'Old Adam' in *As You Like It* ('Think of having Shakespeare in one's arms!' gushed Coleridge of the scene in which Orlando enters carrying him), the ailing John of Gaunt in *Richard II*, and the Ghost of Old Hamlet. In addition to these extended cameos, a slightly better documented tradition assigns him a line in Emperors and Kings – presumably the 'kingly parts' later celebrated by the Hereford poet John Davies in 1610 (below), and perhaps acknowledged in one of his own Sonnets. 'Thus have I had thee as a dream doth flatter,' he writes to the young man: 'In sleep a king, but waking no such matter' (Sonnet 87). The sentiment is one his Christopher Sly would have recognized – and was elaborated in a speech he gave to Burbage as another king, Richard II (below).

Of the stereotypical parts Hamlet lists below, Shakespeare's acting range may have extended to the occasional 'Humorous Man', in particular the jealous cuckold Thorello in one of Jonson's early satires. (The name probably stayed in his mind when he wrote *Othello*.) Otherwise, he seems to have reserved something of an ironic gaze for the roles of 'Adventurous Knight' and 'Lover', and a sterner view of the 'Clown' (see p. 51), though he maintained a constant admiration for the boy-actors who played his increasingly complex female leads. An early example of this can be seen in the Fourth Act of *The Two Gentlemen of Verona*, where Julia, played by a boy, and now disguised as Sebastian, confesses to having once dressed up in Julia's clothing and played 'the woman's part' on a stage.

Hamlet (1600–1), 2.2:

HAMLET. Why did you laugh then when I said man
   delights not me?

ROSENCRANTZ. To think, my lord, if you delight not in
man, what °lenten entertainment the players shall
receive from you. We °coted them on the way, and
hither are they coming to offer you service.

HAMLET. He that plays the King shall be welcome — His
Majesty shall have tribute from me; the Adventurous
Knight shall use his °foil and target; the Lover shall not
sigh gratis; the Humorous Man shall °end his part in
peace; the Clown shall make those laugh whose lungs
are °tickle o' the sear; and the Lady shall say her mind
freely — or the blank verse shall °halt for't.

John Davies of Hereford, 'To our English °Terence Mr. Will:
Shake-speare': *The Scourge of Folly*, 1610, Epigram 159:

Some say, good Will — which I, in sport, do sing —
Hadst thou not play'd some kingly parts in sport,
Thou hadst been a companion for a King
And been a king among the meaner sort.
Some others °rail; but, rail as they think fit,
Thou hast no railing but a reigning wit.
And °honesty thou sow'st, which they do reap,
So to increase their stock which they do keep.

Richard II (1595), 5.5:

RICHARD. Thus play I in one person many people,
And none contented. Sometimes am I king;
Then treasons make me wish myself a beggar,
And so I am. Then crushing penury
Persuades me I was better when a king.
Then am I king'd again; and by and by
Think that I am unking'd by Bolingbroke,
And straight am nothing. But whate'er I be,
Nor I nor any man that but man is
With nothing shall be pleas'd, till he be eas'd
With being nothing.

The Two Gentlemen of Verona (1593), 4.4:

SILVIA. How tall was she?

JULIA (*disguised as* SEBASTIAN).
  About my stature; for at °Pentecost,
  When all our pageants of delight were play'd,
  Our youth got me to play the woman's part,
  And I was trimm'd in Madam Julia's gown,
  Which served me as fit, by all men's judgements,
  As if the garment had been made for me:
  Therefore I know she is about my height.
  And at that time I made her weep agood,
  For I did play a lamentable part.

'All the world's a stage'

Opinion still divides over which of Shakespeare's plays it was that opened his company's new Bankside theatre in the summer of 1599. If it was the History of *Henry V*, the mustering energies of its Chorus would have repeatedly drawn an audience's attention to the auspices of the 'wooden O'. If it was the Tragedy of *Julius Caesar* (certainly in repertoire that September), the setting would have finessed the sense in which London's ever-grander playhouses emulated the grandeur and eminence of Ancient Rome, with their imitation marble pillars and classical pedigree. But if it was the Comedy of *As You Like It*, Jaques's centrepiece speech, soon famous, would first have been heard as a testimonial to, and advertisement for, the unparalleled range of the company's actors, and as a thrilling manifesto for the great Globe itself.

As You Like It (1599–1600), 2.7:

DUKE SENIOR. Thou seest we are not all alone unhappy:
  This wide and universal theatre
  Presents more woeful pageants than the scene
  Wherein we play in.

JAQUES.   All the world's a stage,
   And all the men and women merely players:
   They have their exits and their entrances;
   And one man in his time plays many parts,
   His acts being seven ages. At first the infant,
   Mewling and puking in the nurse's arms.
   And then the whining schoolboy, with his satchel
   And shining morning face, creeping like snail
   Unwillingly to school. And then the lover,
   Sighing like furnace, with a woeful ballad
   Made to his mistress' eyebrow. Then a soldier,
   Full of strange oaths and bearded like the °pard,
   Jealous in honour, sudden and quick in quarrel,
   Seeking the bubble reputation
   Even in the cannon's mouth. And then the justice,
   In fair round belly with good capon lin'd,
   With eyes severe and beard of formal cut,
   Full of wise °saws and modern instances;
   And so he plays his part. The sixth age shifts
   Into the lean and slipper'd °pantaloon,
   With spectacles on nose and °pouch on side,
   His youthful °hose, well sav'd, a world too wide
   For his shrunk shank; and his big manly voice,
   Turning again toward childish treble, pipes
   And whistles in his sound. Last scene of all,
   That ends this strange eventful history,
   Is second childishness and mere oblivion,
   °Sans teeth, sans eyes, sans taste, sans everything.

Shakespeare's career in the theatre was played out against the constant backdrop of censure by the Puritan authorities of London, which is why all the playhouses were located beyond the City boundaries (in Shoreditch and Clerkenwell to the north, and Bankside on the south side of the Thames). To such critics, the daily impersonation that is the actor's stock-in-trade represented a pagan affront to the God-given social hierarchy, inciting violence and lust in the spectator, and the divine retribution of plague. Fellow dramatist

Thomas Heywood's take on Shakespeare's most famous speech, which prefaces his extended essay *An Apology for Actors*, is therefore careful to introduce, along with an appropriately formal rhyme scheme, the pious feature so conspicuously lacking from Jaques's bleak appraisal of the human condition: the presence of God, as both the casting director and prime spectator of our 'universal theatre'. As Heywood's own marginal gloss to his closing couplet summarizes the case, 'No theatre, no world'.

from Thomas Heywood, *An Apology for Actors* (1613):

The world's a theatre, the earth a stage,
Which God and Nature doth with actors fill:
Kings have their entrance in due °equipage,
And some their parts play well, and others ill.
The best no better are in this theatre,
Where every humour's fitted in his kind:
This a true subject acts, and that a traitor,
The first applauded and the last confin'd;
This plays an honest man, and that a knave,
A gentle person this, and he a clown;
One man is raggèd, and another °brave;
All men have parts, and each man acts his own.
She a chaste lady acteth all her life,
A wanton courtesan another plays:
This covets marriage-love, that nuptial strife,
Both in continual action spend their days.
Some citizens, some soldiers, born to adventure,
Shepherds and sea-men — then our play's begun
When we are born and to the world first enter,
And all find exits when their parts are done.
If then the world a theatre present,
As by the roundness it appears most fit,
Built with star-galleries of high ascent,
In which Jehove doth as spectator sit,
And chief determiner to applaud the best,
And their endeavours crown with more than merit,
But by their evil actions dooms the rest,

To end disgrac'd whilst others praise inherit —
He that denies, then, theatres should be,
He may as well deny a world to me.

'Tomorrow...'

Heywood's argument in defence of the theatrical profession
cut no ice with its critics, who still viewed the playhouses as 'a
continual monument of London's prodigality and folly'. His
pamphlet sponsored a specific *Refutation* (1615), which charac-
terized all actors by the 'parts they play' – a sordid catalogue of
'Treachers, Murderers, Swaggerers, Knaves, Drabs, Queans,
Whores, Bawds, Courtesans, Rogues, Villains, Vagabonds,
Thieves, Rovers, Pirates, Cozeners, Cheaters –' to quote a
small proportion of the list – 'and finally contemners of God
His laws, and the King's, and blasphemers of his holy name,
with such like of infinite variety.' Shakespeare himself variously
reflected (or deflected) the Puritan contempt for his livelihood
in such complex figures as the mean-spirited steward Malvolio
in *Twelfth Night* or the austere hypocrite Angelo in *Measure for
Measure*. Interestingly, however, some of the finest anti-the-
atrical polemic in the period can be found in *Antony and
Cleopatra* – the play inadvertently quoted in the *Refutation* ('Age
cannot wither her, nor custom stale / Her *infinite variety*'). Following Antony's protracted suicide, and her own capture by
Octavius Caesar, Cleopatra bitterly anticipates her public exhi-
bition in the streets of Rome (and of course her impersonation
on a future stage by the child-actor now speaking these lines –
and so 'boy[ing] her greatness').

Antony and Cleopatra (1607), 5.2:

CLEOPATRA.   Now, Iras, what think'st thou?
   Thou an Egyptian °puppet shall be shown
   In Rome as well as I. °Mechanic slaves
   With greasy aprons, rules, and hammers, shall
   Uplift us to the view. In their thick breaths,

Rank of gross diet, shall we be enclouded
And forc'd to drink their vapour.

IRAS. The gods forbid!

CLEOPATRA. Nay, 'tis most certain, Iras: °saucy lictors
Will catch at us, like strumpets, and scald rhymers
Ballad us out o' tune; the quick comedians
Extemporally will stage us, and present
Our Alexandrian revels; Antony
Shall be brought drunken forth, and I shall see
Some squeaking Cleopatra boy my greatness
I' th' posture of a whore.

'... and tomorrow...'

Like Shakespeare's own company, Peter Quince and his fellow
'mechanicals' (brethren to the 'Mechanic slaves' so disdained
by Cleopatra) are forced to rehearse their play 'a mile without
the town', and beyond the city walls.

A Midsummer Night's Dream (1595), 1.2:

QUINCE. But masters, here are your parts, and I am to
entreat you, request you, and desire you, to °con them
by tomorrow night: and meet me in the palace wood, a
mile without the town, by moonlight; there will we
rehearse, for if we meet in the city, we shall be dogged
with company, and our devices known. In the
meantime, I will draw a °bill of properties such as our
play wants. I pray you fail me not.

BOTTOM. We will meet, and there we may rehearse more
°obscenely and courageously. Take pains, be perfect,
adieu!

QUINCE. At the Duke's oak we meet.

'… and tomorrow'

For all the infinite multiplicity of parts that a man or woman might be assigned to play on the stage of their life, the curtain must eventually fall on it. And that is the bleak force of what is probably Shakespeare's most concentrated and nihilistic vision of the world's constantly emptying stage. Perhaps inspired by the government's sporadic closure of the London theatres in the wake of renewed outbreaks of plague and the Gunpowder Plot in November 1605, and the forlorn spectacle (as we say these days) of their 'going dark', Macbeth's speech reimagines the daily grind of a lowly actor's career, and the poetry of his ephemeral words, as a momentary and meaningless commotion on an unobserved and neglected stage.

Macbeth (1606), 5.5:

MACBETH. Tomorrow, and tomorrow, and tomorrow
　　Creeps in this petty pace from day to day
　　To the last syllable of recorded time,
　　And all our yesterdays have lighted fools
　　The way to dusty death. Out, out, brief candle!
　　Life's but a walking shadow, a poor player
　　That struts and frets his hour upon the stage
　　And then is heard no more. It is a tale
　　Told by an idiot, full of sound and fury,
　　Signifying nothing.

2

Learning Lines
and Rehearsing Roles

Nature few actors for themselves explore:
They copy those who copied them before.

Anon. (1810)

VANDAMM. Has anyone ever told you that you overplay
your various roles rather severely, Mr Kaplan? It
seems to me you fellows could stand a little less
training from the FBI and a little more from the
Actors Studio.

ROGER. Apparently, the only performance that will
satisfy you is when I play dead.

VANDAMM. Your very next role.

North by Northwest (1959)

Actors these days generally learn their lines from paperback
editions of old plays, or laser-printed scripts of new ones
– their own parts typically highlighted in marker-pen.
Rehearsals tend to be largely group endeavours, at the very
least involving the principals of any scene, and generally sched-
uled over a concentrated period of days or weeks before the
opening night of a play's run. All this is a far cry from how
things were ordered in Shakespeare's theatre, where the bill
changed every day, and when the first long run in English theatrical history (in August 1624, at the Globe) amounted to an

astounding nine successive days. Collective rehearsal was therefore a more rudimentary affair, primarily concerned with blocking, stage-business, and such specialist 'effects' as group dances, sword-play, and battle-scenes, when the company's 'Hired Men' would be put through their paces. (These were the bit-part actors and musicians employed on a freelance basis and contract rate by the company's 'Sharers', the permanent members who received a portion of overall profits in return for their investment and work.) Having memorized their roles from their individual cue-scripts, up-and-coming actors might receive one-to-one tuition on individual speeches from the author (for a new play), or a previously successful actor in the part (for an old one), imparting the appropriate inflections, 'dialect, and different skill' – as Shakespeare put it in *A Lover's Complaint* – 'Catching all passions in his craft of will' (1609).

Given the demands of such a schedule, it is possible that the only time most of the actors involved in a new play would have heard the full script from start to finish before its première was at its original read-through. (Henslowe's Diary records a number of payments for such events, held in a local pub.) It has therefore sometimes been argued that, since the actors had only memorized the cue-lines for their own speeches, and were therefore largely unfamiliar with the content of their fellow actors' lines, a play's production may have gained heightened effect from the semi-improvised nature of its first complete, collective performance.

A working actor's life was in any case dominated by the daily grind of learning the lines of a new part, or else refreshing his memory of an old one, and the carefully labelled scrolls of each man's repertoire were constantly to hand. This is literally so in the case of *Julius Caesar*, where it has been noticed that the assassination scene (3.1), with the full company on stage, each clutching the scroll of their petition, startlingly resembles a group rehearsal of its own staging. (The effect is enhanced by Cassius's question afterwards, as forceful today as it was in 1599: 'How many ages hence / Shall this our lofty scene be acted over / In states unborn and accents yet unknown?') That visual pun – and the larger sense in which global history is being made by an under-rehearsed group of power-players, semi-improvising their roles as they go along – matches a series of verbal echoes in other of Shakespeare's scripts, persistent reminders of the theatrical auspices of the stories they tell. 'The copy of your speed is learn'd by them,' reports a lowly Messenger to King John, transposing the military strategy of a forced march to the equally arduous business of another sort of troupe – as heartfelt a description as that made in *A Midsummer Night's Dream* by the Master of Revels at Duke Theseus's court, who describes the mechanicals' forthcoming production as one 'conn'd with cruel pain, / To do you service'.

The empty space

In Shakespeare's day, a play's première at the public theatre technically remained a dress rehearsal for the censor, in advance of his passing it as suitable for its private performance at court – which is the precise circumstance of the mechanicals' excruciating *Pyramus and Thisbe*, 'Which, when I saw rehears'd,' as Philostrate, the Master of Revels, tells Duke Theseus, 'I must confess / Made mine eyes water' (5.1). As Quince observes, the clearing in the woods beyond the city walls (and the real stage and tiring-house he indicates, likewise situated beyond the jurisdiction of the city) provided a useful rehearsal space.

A Midsummer Night's Dream (1595), 3.1:

BOTTOM. Are we all met?

QUINCE. Pat, pat, and here's a marvellous convenient place for our rehearsal. This green plot shall be our stage, this hawthorn °brake our tiring-house, and we will do it in action, as we will do it before the Duke.

Director's notes

Given the pragmatic logistics of a professional Elizabethan actor's working life, rehearsals in a role generally conformed to a stereotypical approach to his part ('What is Pyramus?' asks Bottom, 'A Lover or a Tyrant?'), and Shakespeare seems to have preferred a generic description of his characters ahead of their names as he wrote. The actual names of King Claudius in *Hamlet* and Duke Vincentio in *Measure for Measure* are never spoken on stage, for example, and in the working papers of *All's Well That Ends Well*, later printed in the First Folio, the Countess is variously referred to as 'Mother', 'Old Countess', and 'Old Lady', while the stage-directions in the Quarto text of *Romeo and Juliet* likewise characterize Lady Capulet as a succession of her social roles. Such labelling usefully prompted an off-the-peg style of casting and acting: the character 'types' would have helped determine who in the company played what – the skinny John Sincklo, for example, cornering the market in such parts as the slender Feeble in *Henry IV, Part Two* and the feeble Slender in *The Merry Wives of Windsor*. (Such a scheme persisted from such stock characters as Harlequin or Pantaloon in the sixteenth-century *Commedia dell'Arte* to the 'juve' – or juvenile lead – in the 'rep' companies of the twentieth.) 'Faith, we can say our parts,' remarks a nervous player to the director in one of Marston's Inductions, 'but we are ignorant in what mould we must cast our actors [= *characters*]' (*Antonio and Mellida*, 1600). At the same time, however, Shakespeare helped his company pioneer a brand-new trademark naturalism, famously recommended in Hamlet's advice to the Players in advance of their court performance.

Hamlet (1600–1), 3.2:

HAMLET. Speak the speech, I pray you, as I pronounced it
to you, trippingly on the tongue: but if you mouth it,
as many of your players do, I had as °lief the town-crier
spoke my lines. Nor do not saw the air too much with
your hand, thus, but use all gently; for in the very

torrent, tempest, and, as I may say, the whirlwind of your passion, you must acquire and °beget a temperance that may give it smoothness. O, it offends me to the soul to hear a °robustious periwig-pated fellow °tear a passion to tatters, to very rags, to split the ears of the °groundlings, who for the most part are capable of nothing but inexplicable Dumb Shows and noise: I would have such a fellow whipped for °o'erdoing Termagant; it out-Herods Herod. Pray you, avoid it.

1 PLAYER. I °warrant your honour.

HAMLET. Be not too tame neither, but let your own discretion be your tutor: suit the action to the word, the word to the action; with this special observance, that you o'erstep not the modesty of nature: for anything so overdone is from the purpose of playing, whose end, both at the first and now, was and is, to hold, as 'twere, the mirror up to Nature — to show Virtue her own feature, Scorn her own image, and the very age and body of the time his °form and pressure. Now this overdone, or come tardy off, though it make the unskilful laugh, cannot but make the judicious grieve, the censure of which one must in your allowance o'erweigh a whole theatre of others. O, there be players that I have seen play — and heard others praise, and that highly — not to speak it profanely, that, neither having the accent of Christians nor the gait of Christian, pagan, nor man, have so strutted and bellowed that I have thought some of Nature's °journeymen had made men and not made them well, they imitated humanity so abominably.

1 PLAYER. I hope we have reformed that °indifferently with us, sir.

HAMLET. O, reform it altogether, and let those that play your clowns speak no more than is set down for them. For there be of them that will themselves laugh to set on some quantity of °barren spectators to laugh too,

though in the meantime some necessary question of
the play be then to be considered. That's villainous,
and shows a most pitiful ambition in the fool that uses
it. Go, make you ready.

Exeunt PLAYERS.

Ham acting

Hamlet's 'notes' are rare for including a few choice positive tips
among the slew of negative advice that elsewhere colours
Shakespeare's directorial approach (some of which are collected below under 'Fluffs, Prompts, Cues, and Snags', pp.
127–144). Their general tenor amounts to a plea for restraint.
The words of the script should be delivered lightly and fluently
('trippingly'), never declaimed ('if you mouth it'); even at the
height or depth of a hero's emotional journey, 'temperance' in
a performance will lend credibility and 'give it smoothness'.
Less is more – and the same goes for the company Clown. It's
all too easy to hog the limelight by grabbing a cheap laugh, but
such improvised comic business can shatter the balance of a
play's rhythm and sense. Of course, there are dangers in
underplaying a role too ('Be not too tame neither'), but the
central ideal of Hamlet's critique is a natural realism ('the
modesty of nature') – and the central object of his complaint
is the grandiloquent style of the Globe's neighbours and rivals
at the Rose, the Lord Admiral's Men.

    The leading actor of the Admiral's company was Edward
Alleyn, who achieved fame and fortune in the early 1590s by
pioneering the performance of Marlowe's 'over-reaching' anti-
heroes, roles he continued to revive into the new century. By
the time the Chamberlain's Men built the Globe in 1599,
however, Alleyn's acting style had come to feel old-fashioned
– or so Shakespeare's Hamlet, first played by Richard Burbage,
implies. Just as Shakespeare's scripts had come to modulate
Marlowe's thunderous style, adding human dimension to his
'mighty line', so Burbage had introduced a subtler pitch to his

characterization. Whoever it was that put together *Hamlet*'s bootlegged First Quarto (1603) deepened the rivalrous insult by likening the ham actor's bombast, not to the shouting 'town-crier' of the authoritative text, but to a bellowing 'town-bull'. John Marston meanwhile ridiculed a player's formulaic representation of grief ('Wouldst have me... Stamp, curse, weep, rage, and then my bosom strike? / Away, 'tis apeish action, player-like!'), and Shakespeare himself burlesqued the style in Ulysses' bitter description of Patroclus' insolent impersonation of Agamemnon, where bad acting is rendered tantamount to lack of moral fibre.

Troilus and Cressida (1601–2), 1.3:

ULYSSES. The great Achilles, whom opinion crowns
    The °sinew and the forehand of our host,
    Having his ear full of his airy fame,
    Grows °dainty of his worth, and in his tent
    Lies mocking our designs. With him Patroclus,
    Upon a lazy bed, the livelong day
    °Breaks scurril jests,
    And with ridiculous and awkward action
    (Which, slanderer, he 'imitation' calls)
    He °pageants us. Sometime, great Agamemnon,
    °Thy topless deputation he puts on,
    And, like a strutting player whose conceit
    Lies in his hamstring, and doth think it rich
    To hear the wooden dialogue and sound
    'Twixt his stretch'd footing and the scaffoldage,
    Such to-be-pitied and °o'er-wrested seeming
    He acts thy greatness in; and when he speaks,
    'Tis like a °chime a-mending, with terms unsquar'd,
    Which from the tongue of roaring °Typhon dropp'd
    Would seem hyperboles. At this °fusty stuff
    The large Achilles, on his press'd bed lolling,
    From his deep chest laughs out a loud applause,
    Cries 'Excellent! 'tis Agamemnon just.'

Such practical examples of 'How Not To Act' are furthered by Thomas Nashe, in his playful Induction to *Summer's Last Will and Testament*, where the ghost of the dead court jester Will Summers presides over a pageant of seasonal – and human – transience. Albeit the Elizabethan equivalent of Spencer Tracy's 'Know your lines and don't bump into the furniture', the advice holds good to this day.

from Thomas Nashe, *Summer's Last Will and Testament* (1592), Prologue:

WILL SUMMERS. Actors, you rogues, come away! Clear your throats, blow your noses, and wipe your mouths ere you enter, that you may take no occasion to spit or cough when you are *non-plus*. And this I bar, over and besides: that none of you stroke your beards to make action, play with your °codpiece points, or stand fumbling with your buttons when you know not how to bestow your fingers. Serve God, and act cleanly.

Repeat after me...

It is clear from Hamlet's advice to the Players that he has personally coached them in the required delivery ('Speak the speech... as I pronounced it to you') before the scene began. This seems to have been a common practice – the so-called 'instruction' by which an author talked through a role with his lead, or a successful actor passed on the techniques of his performance of a part to his protégé. Versions of such tutorials repeatedly surface in Shakespeare's plays, and in a variety of imagined tutorials: the tyrant usurper Richard to his eager accomplice, for example; or the elderly spy-master Polonius to his junior agent.

Richard III (1594), 3.5:

RICHARD.
> Come, cousin, canst thou quake and change thy colour,
> °Murder thy breath in middle of a word,
> And then again begin, and stop again,
> As if thou were distraught and mad with terror?

BUCKINGHAM. Tut, I can counterfeit the deep tragedian,
> Speak, and look back, and pry on every side,
> Tremble and start at °wagging of a straw,
> °Intending deep suspicion. Ghastly looks
> Are at my service, like enforcèd smiles,
> And both are ready in their offices
> At any time to grace my stratagems.

Hamlet (1600–1), 2.1:

POLONIUS.
> Take you as 'twere some distant knowledge of him,
> As thus: 'I know his father and his friends,
> And in part him. —' Do you mark this, Reynaldo?

REYNALDO. Ay, very well, my lord.

POLONIUS.
> '— And in part him. But —' you may say — 'not well;
> But if't be he I mean, he's very wild,
> Addicted,' so and so: and there put on him
> What forgeries you please. Marry, none so rank
> As may dishonour him (take heed of that)
> But, sir, such wanton, wild, and usual slips
> As are companions noted and most known
> To youth and liberty.

REYNALDO.   As gaming, my lord?

POLONIUS. Ay, or drinking, fencing, swearing,
> Quarrelling, °drabbing — you may go so far.

Dismissed by some as mere 'leaden spouts… That nought do vent but what they do receive' (see above, p. 38), it wasn't only Puritan bureaucrats and university scholars who resented the conspicuous rise in profile and wealth enjoyed by Elizabethan actors. Poets did, too. John Davies contrasted the peacock finery of a player's costume with their witless parroting of others' words.

from John Davies of Hereford, *Microcosmos: The Discovery of the Little World* (1603):

> But that which grates my gall and mads my Muse
> Is — ah, that ever such just cause should be! —
> To see a player at the °put-down stews
> Put up his peacock's tail for all to see,
> And for his hellish voice as proud as he.
> What, peacock, art thou proud? Wherefore? Because
> Thou parrot-like canst speak what is taught thee?
> A poet must teach thee from clause to clause
> Or thou will break pronunciation's laws.
>
> Lies all thy virtue in thy tongue °still taught,
> And yet art proud? Alas, poor scum of Pride! [...]
> Base Pride, didst thou thyself or others know,
> Wouldst thou in hearts of apeish actors lie,
> That for a cue will sell their °quality?
> Yet they through thy persuasion (being strong)
> Do °ween they merit immortality
> Only because, forsooth, they use their tongue
> To speak as they are taught, or right or wrong.

Whose line is it anyway?

Shakespeare seems to have pioneered our modern sense of individual authorship, and of a play's internal thematic integrity. When he began his career, most plays were either updatings of pre-existing scripts, jointly revised by a succession of actors and writers, or else collaborative endeavours by professional dramatists, such as those commissioned by Henslowe at the Rose. As many as five different playwrights – like 'cart*wright*' or 'wheel-*wright*', the term is suggestive of a functional craft – are known to have worked on a single play, and it is by no means always clear that the author of a final scene had ever read anything more than a synopsis of the first. This way of working particularly affected the company Clown, who was expected to improvise a routine at specific points in the action. Launce's shtick with his dog in *The Two Gentlemen of Verona*, Peter's guying of the three musicians in *Romeo and Juliet*, and Launcelot Gobbo's ridicule of his deaf father in *The Merchant of Venice* may all be versions of such routines devised by Will Kemp, the founder member (with Burbage and Shakespeare) of the Lord Chamberlain's Men, refined and polished into the finished script. For some reason, however, relations between Kemp and the rest of the company did not long survive their transfer to the Globe in 1599 – possibly in part because its principal dramatist restricted the opportunity for Kemp's improvisational patter in his increasingly single-minded plays. It is telling, for example, that Hamlet ends his 'notes' with a warning to clowns not to speak 'more than is set down for them'. Intriguingly, the same passage in the play's illicit First Quarto edition (below) seems to incorporate a set of additional specific routines ('And then you have some again...') from the stand-up's joke-book, of the sort specifically forbidden in Shakespeare's original script.

Hamlet, First Quarto (1603), 2.2:

HAMLET. And do you hear? Let not your clown speak
    more than is set down. There be of them, I can tell
    you, that will laugh themselves to set on some quantity
    of barren spectators to laugh with them, albeit there is
    some necessary point in the play then to be observed.
    O, 'tis vile, and shows a pitiful ambition in the fool that
    useth it. And then you have some again that keeps one
    °suit of jests as a man is known by one suit of apparel,
    and gentlemen quote his jests down in their °tables
    before they come to the play, as thus: 'Cannot you stay
    till I eat my porridge?' And 'You owe me a quarter's
    wages'; and 'My coat wants a °cullison'; and 'Your beer
    is sour', and blabbering with his lips — and thus
    keeping a °cinquepace of jests when, God knows, the

°warm clown cannot make a jest unless by chance, as
the blind man catcheth a hare. Masters, tell him of it.

As Octavius Caesar says in a different context, 'Do not exceed
/ The prescript of this scroll' (*Antony and Cleopatra*, 1607, 3.8).
Hamlet describes such a Clown's flagrant scene-stealing as
'vile' ('villainous' in the authoritative Second Quarto), an opinion lengthily shared (below) by the theatrical patron Lord
Letoy in Richard Brome's *The Antipodes* (1638). Despite dating
from nearly forty years later, it is remarkable how closely he
sticks to the tenor of Hamlet's advice in instructing his company. Letoy begins by commending his leading actor, Byplay,
who compensates for his terrible memory for lines by the bril-
liance of his quick-witted improvisations; then he gives a
detailed set of 'notes' to the other actors (essentially listing a set
of bad habits that seem to have returned during final
rehearsals), before sternly addressing Byplay himself on the
'barbarism' of his technique, reminiscent, he says, of the dis-
ruptive 'days of Tarlton and Kemp'. (In fact, however, Byplay's
improvised interaction with the audience turns out to be precisely what's required of him.)

Richard Brome, *The Antipodes* (1638), 2.1:

LETOY.   Well, sir, my actors
　Are all in readiness; and, I think, all perfect
　But one, that never will be perfect in a thing
　He studies. Yet he makes such shifts extempore,
　Knowing the purpose what he is to speak to,
　That he moves mirth in me 'bove all the rest.
　For I am none of these poetic furies
　That threats an actor's life in a whole play
　That adds a syllable or takes away. [...]

Enter BYPLAY *and other* ACTORS.

(*To them.*)   Let me not see you act now
　In your scholastic way you brought to town wi' ye,
　With °seesaw sack-a-down, like a sawyer,
　Nor in a comic scene play °*Hercules Furens*,

Tearing your throat to split the °audients' ears. —
And you, sir, you had got the trick of late
Of holding out your bum in a set speech,
Your fingers fibulating on your breast
As if your buttons or your °band-strings were
Helps to your memory. Let me see you in't
No more, I charge you. — No, nor you, sir, in
That over-action of your legs I told you of. [...]
— And when you have spoke, at end of every speech,
Not minding the reply, you turn you round
As tumblers do, when betwixt every feat
They °gather wind by firking up their breeches.
I'll none of these absurdities in my house,
But words and actions married so together
That shall strike harmony in the ears and eyes
Of the severest, if judicious, critics. [...]
(*To* BYPLAY.) But you, sir, are incorrigible, and
Take licence to yourself to add unto
Your parts your own free fancy; and sometimes
To alter or diminish what the writer
With care and skill compos'd. And when you are
To speak to your co-actors in the scene,
You hold °interlocutions with the °audients.

BYPLAY. That is a way, my lord, has been allow'd
On elder stages to move mirth and laughter.

LETOY. Yes, in the days of Tarlton and Kemp,
Before the stage was purg'd from barbarism
And brought to the perfection it now shines with.
Then fools and jesters °spent their wits because
The poets were wise enough to save their own
For profitabler uses. Let that pass.
Tonight I'll give thee leave to try thy wit.

'Premeditated lines'

The lapses of Byplay's imperfect memory were an occupa-
tional hazard for actors on Shakespeare's stage (and the ability
to invent a few lines of cod-Elizabethan blank verse to fill in
for a late cue or botched effect remains a useful skill for actors
today). In order to reduce that burden, it seems to have been a
common practice for the company copyist to transcribe the
many letters, proclamations, poems, and other texts recited on
stage in the form of prop-scrolls, which were indeed read out
rather than memorized by the relevant performers. This is why
the earliest Quarto edition of Kyd's *Spanish Tragedy* (1592)
inadvertently reproduced the author's (or book-keeper's)
instruction '*Red ink*' as a marginal stage-direction when
Hieronymo receives a letter written in blood – and also why
such recitations are so often distinguished, with a larger or an
italic font, in a play's early printed texts. Shakespeare is probably playing with this established convention in the central
scene of *Henry VI, Part One*, where one character enters with
what seems to be just such a crib (in the form of a written
charge-sheet), which is then immediately snatched away and
ripped up on stage by his rival.

Henry VI, Part One (1592) 3.1:

> *Flourish. Enter the* KING [*and his Lords to Parliament*]. *The*
> DUKE OF GLOUCESTER *offers to put up a bill; the* BISHOP
> OF WINCHESTER *snatches it, tears it.*

WINCHESTER. Com'st thou with deep premeditated lines,
    With written pamphlets studiously devis'd?
    Humphrey of Gloucester, if thou canst accuse,
    Or aught intend'st to lay unto my charge,
    Do it without invention, suddenly,
    As I with sudden and extemporal speech
    Purpose to answer what thou canst object.

GLOUCESTER. Presumptuous priest! This place
      commands my patience,
    Or thou shouldst find thou hast dishonour'd me.

Think not, although in writing I °preferr'd
The manner of thy vile outrageous crimes,
That therefore I have forg'd or am not able
Verbatim to rehearse the method of my pen.

Meanwhile, the actors playing these lines would have learned and rehearsed them from the individual scrolls, or part-scripts, that had been copied out by the company scribe and distributed in advance of the play's première. One such script – the title role in Robert Greene's *Orlando Furioso* – has survived in the archives of Dulwich College, the school that its original owner, Edward Alleyn, founded in 1619. The following extracts, modernized from these precious documents – and from the published Quarto edition later made of the whole play – illustrate the daily practice of an Elizabethan working actor.

Greene's play makes two claims to literary fame. The first is Shakespeare's borrowing both of its hero's name for *As You Like It* and the idea of his posting love-verses on the trees of a forest (though in Greene's play they are wicked forgeries intended to drive Orlando mad). The second is the famous piece of sharp practice by which Greene managed to sell exclusive rights in this play to two different companies at the same time – which may explain the discrepancy between Alleyn's part-script and the 1594 Quarto. (The isolated words at the end of the long lines below are the 'cue-words' – i.e. the last words of the speeches spoken by others in the scene, which accordingly cue the next exchange.) The first of these extracts is perhaps the closest we can come to seeing the form in which Shakespeare first encountered his roles in the early parts he played; the second anticipates the textual tangles and rewordings that many of his own plays underwent on their journey between stage and print.

from Alleyn's cue-script to Robert Greene, *Orlando Furioso* (c. 1591):

ARGALIO.

—————————————————————— My lord.
Come hither, Argalio. Villain, behold these lines:
See all these trees, carv'd with true love-knots
Wherein are figur'd 'Medor' and 'Angelica'.
What think'st thou of it?
—————————————————————— is a woman.
And what then?
—————————————————————— some news.
What messenger hath °Ate sent abroad
With idle looks to listen my lament?
Sirrah, who wrongèd happy Nature thus
To spoil these trees with this 'Angelica'?
Yet in her name, Orlando, they are blest.
—————————————————————— follow love.
As follow love? Dar'st thou dispraise my heaven?

from Robert Greene, *Orlando Furioso* (1594):

ORLANDO. Orgalio!

ORGALIO. My lord?

ORLANDO. Boy, view these trees, carv'd with true love-
        knots,
    The inscription 'Medor and Angelica',
    And read these verses hung up of their loves.
    Now tell me, boy, what dost thou think?

ORGALIO. By my troth, my lord, I think Angelica is a
    woman.

ORLANDO. And what of that?

ORGALIO. Therefore unconstant, mutable, having their
    loves hanging in their eyelids; that as they are °got
    with a look, so they are lost again with a wink.

    Enter a SHEPHERD.

    But here's a shepherd. It may be he can tell us news.

ORLANDO. What messenger hath °Ate sent abroad
  With idle looks to listen my laments?
  Sirrah, who wrongèd happy Nature thus
  To spoil these trees with this 'Angelica'?
  (*Aside.*) Yet in her name, Orlando, they are blest.

SHEPHERD. I am a shepherd swain, thou wand'ring knight,
  That watch my flocks — not one that follow love.

ORLANDO. [Not] follow love?
  Why darest thou dispraise my heaven?

Snug the joiner (below) has even less faith in his ability to learn lines than Brome's Byplay ('I am slow of study'), but Quince's reassurance on the wholly improvisational nature of his role – no need for any cue-script for Snug – prompts yet another impromptu audition from Bottom. For some reason, actors had a reputation for ruthlessly competing for plum roles. 'We're not factious, / Or envy one another for best parts,' says the casting director of an amateur masque, somewhat ruefully, in Thomas Middleton's *No Wit Like a Woman's*, 'Like quarrelling actors that have passionate fits. / We submit always to the writer's wits' (1611, scene 7). Some hope.

A Midsummer Night's Dream (1595), 1.2:

SNUG. Have you the lion's part written? Pray you if it be, give it me, for I am slow of study.

QUINCE. You may do it extempore, for it is nothing but roaring.

BOTTOM. Let me play the lion too — I will roar that I will do any man's heart good to hear me. I will roar that I will make the Duke say, 'Let him roar again, let him roar again!'

QUINCE. If you should do it too terribly, you would fright the Duchess and the ladies, that they would shriek, and that were enough to hang us all.

ALL. That would hang us, every mother's son.

BOTTOM. I grant you, friends, if that you should fright the ladies out of their wits, they would have no more discretion but to hang us. But I will °aggravate my voice so, that I will roar you as gently as any °sucking dove; I will roar you an 'twere any nightingale.

QUINCE. You can play no part but Pyramus, for Pyramus is a sweet-faced man; a proper man as one shall see in a summer's day; a most lovely, gentleman-like man: therefore you must needs play Pyramus.

BOTTOM. Well, I will undertake it.

A choreographer's tantrum

The exasperated patience with which Peter Quince tactfully coaxes his actors towards a performance is a comic routine to which Shakespeare repeatedly returned. Like his fellow directors Holofernes (whose pageant of the Nine – in the event only Five – Worthies concludes *Love's Labour's Lost*) and Hugh Evans (who stage-manages his pupils' impersonation of fairies to complete Falstaff's humiliation in *The Merry Wives of Windsor*), Quince is both well-meaning and rather pompous, with a pronounced liking for the sound of his own voice – provoking the constant suspicion that no one quite knows what he is talking about. The role was reprised in the last play to which Shakespeare contributed. Co-written with John Fletcher, *The Two Noble Kinsmen* includes a scene in which another Welsh schoolteacher, Gerald, is struggling to teach a group of baffled countrymen the moves of a complicated dance, planned for performance before another Duke Theseus. They are still stuck on how to make their entrance when the scene opens.

The Two Noble Kinsmen (1613), 3.5:

GERALD. Fie, fie, what °tediosity and disinsanity is here among ye? Have my rudiments been laboured so long with ye, °milked unto ye, and (by a °figure) even the very °plum-broth and marrow of my understanding laid upon ye — and do you still cry 'Where?' and 'How?' and 'Wherefore?' You most coarse-frieze capacities, ye lean judgements, have I said 'Thus let be' and 'There let be', and no man understand me? °*Proh Deum! Medius Fidius!* Ye are all dunces! For why? Here stand I. — Here the Duke comes. — There are you, close in the thicket. — The Duke appears. — I meet him, and unto him I utter learned things and many °figures. — He hears and nods and hums and then cries °'Rare!' and I go forward. — At length I fling my cap up — mark, there. — Then do you (as once did °Meleager and the boar) break comely out before him: like true °lovers, cast yourselves in a body decently and sweetly, by a figure, °trace and turn, boys!

1 COUNTRYMAN. And sweetly we will do it, Master Gerald.

Quince's patience, however, is tested beyond even Gerald's breaking point when Bottom misses his cue in rehearsals, watched, invisibly, by Puck.

A Midsummer Night's Dream (1595), 3.1:

QUINCE. Speak, Pyramus. Thisbe, stand forth.

BOTTOM. 'Thisbe, the flowers of odious savours sweet —'

QUINCE. 'Odours'! '*Odours*'!

BOTTOM.   '— *odours* savours sweet:
So hath thy breath, my dearest Thisbe dear.
But hark, a voice. Stay thou but here awhile,
And by and by I will to thee appear.'

                                        Exit BOTTOM.

PUCK (*aside*). A stranger Pyramus than e'er played here!

FLUTE. Must I speak now?

QUINCE. Ay, marry must you. For you must understand he goes but to see a noise that he heard, and is to come again.

FLUTE. 'Most radiant Pyramus, most lily-white of hue,
Of colour like the red rose on triumphant briar;
Most brisky juvenile, and °eke most lovely °jew,
As true as truest horse that yet would never tire.
I'll meet thee, Pyramus, at Ninny's tomb —'

QUINCE. °'*Ninus*' tomb', man! — Why, you must not
speak that yet. That you answer to Pyramus. You speak
all your part at once, cues and all! — Pyramus, enter:
your cue is past: it is '… never tire'.

FLUTE. Oh.
'As true as truest horse that yet would never tire.'

Enter BOTTOM *as Pyramus, transformed with an ass's head.*

BOTTOM. 'If I were fair, Thisbe, I were only thine —'

QUINCE. O monstrous! O strange! We are haunted! Pray,
masters! Fly, masters! Help!

The CLOWNS *all exit.*

3

Props and Costumes, Notes and Rewrites

To prompter many duties more belong
    Than biding at the wing with book in hand.
Of their go-off, come-on, he points the sides,
    By margin letters of °'P.S.', 'O.P.':
Stage properties, stage business, music, band,
    Of stage arcana prompter keeps the key.

John O'Keefe (1826)

Those stilted boys, that burnished chariot,
Lion and woman and the Lord knows what [...]
Players and painted stage took all my love,
And not those things that they were emblems of.

W.B. Yeats (1938)

'Go get us properties,' instructs Mistress Page in *The Merry Wives of Windsor*, 'And tricking for our fairies' (4.4). And the merry husbands duly oblige, exiting to prepare for Falstaff's humiliation by a band of spirits (to be played by a bunch of schoolboys). Their exit through one of the two doors on the back wall of the stage was in fact an entrance to the very place where the appropriate 'tricking' was stored: for, situated directly behind the stage, stood the company dressing-room known as the 'tiring-house' (as in *attire*), which doubled as convenient storage space for their props, costumes, and play-books. Although we have no record of the treasures once stored in the Globe's tiring-house ('Item: one skull for *Hamlet*'?), we do, astonishingly, have the next-best thing, in the shape of an 'Inventory taken of all the properties... apparel... [and] all such books as belong to the stock' drawn up in the late 1590s by Philip Henslowe, the impresario in charge of the Rose. Here we find listed such vivid items as 'Tamburlaine's coat with copper lace', a 'cauldron for *The Jew* [*of Malta*]', and a 'Hell mouth' (presumably for *Doctor Faustus*), as well as the intriguing note that 'Harry the Fifth's doublet [*and*] velvet gown' were now 'gone and lost'. (Might they have been purchased – or pinched – by the rival company for their forthcoming production at the Globe in spring 1599?) Henslowe's inventory must roughly have duplicated that of his new neighbours on Bankside, including such regularly useful props as a 'bedstead', a box-tomb or two, a range of weaponry, pieces of armour, helmets, crowns, and other hats, a number of severed heads ('*Enter Macduff, with Macbeth's head*'), a 'lionskin' and 'bear's skin' (variously useful for Snug and Antigonus), and even a wooden leg – as well as a wardrobe of gorgeous costumes whose cost routinely exceeded the price of a new script.

In a period when the hierarchy of society was calibrated by clothes – from the servants known as 'blue-coats' to the ultimate authority of 'the crown' – Shakespeare was almost uniquely positioned. Vestiges of this system still (just) survive in the different buttoning on men's shirts and women's blouses; in the white of a bride's wedding dress, and the black tie of mourning; in the distinct gowns and wigs worn by modern barristers and judges in a Court of Law; and in the full fig of university graduation ceremonies.* In those days, even the style of a man's beard ('Some like a spade, some like a fork, some square, / Some round, some mow'd like stubble, some stark bare...') located his role in the social fabric, and was accordingly imitated on stage. Such nuanced distinctions were of constant importance in, and to, Shakespeare's career, which

---

* A pamphlet given out at my graduation solemnly explained that the hood of the gown worn by graduating Bachelors of Veterinary Medicine is 'similar to the hood for Bachelor of Medicine, but with more fur'.

began by dressing up (the 'up' was socially conditioned), and went on to include apparently memorable turns as kings (see above, p. 40), before his company's formal promotion to the status of King's Men in 1603. Each of their members was allocated a length of 'scarlet red cloth', to be tailored into formal livery and worn in attendance during James I's ceremonial entry to the City of London in March 1604. Shakespeare happened to be lodging at the time with a husband-and-wife team of 'tire-makers' – manufacturers of 'tricking' hair-extensions, head-dresses, and tiaras – whose products found equal demand at court and on stage.

As royal servants famed for playing Fools and Kings, Shakespeare's company negotiated a constant double-life of surface and substance, truth and imitation, jewellery and paste – and it was for that social and spiritual duplicity that theatre elicited as much outrage as applause. 'You shall see nothing but the adventures of an Amorous Knight, passing from country to country for the love of his Lady, encountering many a terrible monster made of brown paper,' complained the Puritan critic Stephen Gosson in 1582, sneering at 'the mass of expenses in these spectacles that scarce last like shoes of brown paper'. Henslowe's inventory includes at least one 'terrible monster' in the more durable form of a 'dragon in [*Doctor*] *Faustus*', as well as – startlingly – 'the city of Rome', presumably some sort of painted flat for the same play, which might suggest that the Elizabethan stage was slightly less bare of scenery than is sometimes imagined. The fact that no other such aids for 'passing from country to country' are listed, however, indicates that what Hamlet called 'the mind's eye' remained uppermost among its spectacular resources, just as the Chorus to *Henry V* worked on our 'imaginary forces'. (Henslowe's 'city of Rome' can only really have functioned as an elaborate caption, after all.)

The 'books' containing the poetry of those resources were stored in the tiring-house, alongside the doublets, gowns, swords, and crowns that furnished them. These definitive scripts – also known as 'prompt-books' or 'theatre copies' – were the raw material of all subsequent productions. Marked up with the requisite props and stage-effects, it was from these master documents that the individual cue-parts were prepared, and it was here that were recorded the regular revisions, cuts, and rewordings that – for various reasons – accompanied a play's theatrical lifetime. Each of these manuscript packets also bore the signed certificate from the Master of Revels (the state censor in all but name) authorizing its performance – a crucial document to brandish under the noses of provincial bureaucrats when on tour.

It has often been observed that the magic of the theatre is surprisingly close to the flimsy or tawdry. What seem to be Shakespeare's most private reflections on his career, in the Sonnets, dwell both on the deep taint and superficial gloss of its status (Sonnets 110 and 111). From the brown-paper crown used to taunt the Duke of York in one of his earliest plays, to the 'baseless fabric' in one of his last, he remained keenly aware of the essential fragility of his craft, and that the 'spectacles' his plays created do indeed 'scarce last like shoes of brown paper', leaving 'not a rack behind'.

The props basket

It is no accident that in *The Tempest* – probably Shakespeare's most self-consciously theatrical play – the arch-magician Prospero's description to his daughter of their original shipwreck refers to 'garments', 'stuffs', and 'books': 'necessaries' surely of less use to desert-island castaways than to the strolling players who might now exchange the stuffed 'cloak-bags' of their touring luggage ('doublet, hat, hose, all / That answer to them', as Pisanio describes such a bundle in *Cymbeline*) for the permanent tiring-house backstage.

The Tempest (1612), 1.2:

MIRANDA. How came we ashore?

PROSPERO.   By providence divine.
   Some food we had, and some fresh water, that
   A noble Neapolitan, Gonzalo,

Out of his charity — who being then appointed
Master of this design — did give us, with
Rich garments, linens, stuffs, and necessaries
Which since have °steaded much. So, of his gentleness,
Knowing I lov'd my books, he furnish'd me
From mine own library with volumes that
I prize above my dukedom.

Unlike some stage magicians, however, Shakespeare always
relished the opportunity to explain the trick, as when the Duke
of Buckingham stage-manages Richard's show of reluctance at
accepting the crown, by raiding the props basket for a prayer-
book and hiring a couple of walk-ons to enhance the effect...

Richard III (1594), 3.7:

RICHARD. What, tongueless °blocks were they? Would they
    not speak?
   Will not the Mayor then and his brethren come?

BUCKINGHAM. The Mayor is here at hand. °Intend some
    fear;
   Be not you spoke with but by mighty suit.
   And look you get a prayer-book in your hand
   And stand between two churchmen, good my lord,
   For on that ground I'll make a holy °descant.
   And be not easily won to our requests;
   Play the maid's part: °still answer nay, and take it.

... or when the pure novitiate nun Isabella reduces the weighty
apparatus of male power to a collection of tawdry props.

Measure for Measure (1604), 2.2:

ISABELLA.   Well, believe this:
   No ceremony that to great ones °longs,
   Not the King's crown, nor the deputed sword,
   The Marshal's truncheon, nor the Judge's robe,
   Become them with one half so good a grace
   As mercy does.

Just as nowadays an onstage bottle of Scotch will contain nothing stronger than apple-juice or cold tea, so Henslowe's inventory of props at the Rose included two 'marchpanes' (= *marzipan cakes*), presumably the cardboard replicas later listed alongside a set of carved 'wooden pies' in Richard Brome's fictional tiring-house 'survey'.

Richard Brome, *The Antipodes* (1638), 3.1:

BYPLAY. My lord, the mad young gentleman —

JOYLESS.   What of him?

BYPLAY. He has got into our tiring-house amongst us
    And ta'en a strict survey of all our properties:
    Our statues and our images of gods;
    Our planets and our constellations;
    Our giants, monsters, furies, beasts, and bugbears;
    Our helmets, shields, and visors; hairs and beards;
    Our pasteboard marchpanes and our wooden pies —

LETOY. Sirrah, be brief. Be not you now as long
    In telling what he saw as he surveying.

Touring companies had to improvise many of their effects, of course, and could scarcely be expected to lug their entire collection of props by cart from hall to provincial hall. That circumstance helps explain the rather enjoyable request (below) by a visiting actor to his lordly host for a 'shoulder of mutton' as a necessary prop for his company's play. After all, the raw meat used to display the limbs of Doctor Faustus in the final scene of Marlowe's play, 'all torn asunder by the hand of death', could always find a useful afterlife in the company pot, along with a little vinegar seasoning – though as things turn out, that play doesn't feature on the bill.

from The Induction to *The Taming of a Shrew* (1590):

LORD. Now, sirs, go you and make you ready too,
    For you must play as soon as he doth wake.

1 PLAYER (*aside to his fellow*). O, brave! Sirrah Tom, we
    must play before a foolish lord! Come, let's go make us

ready. Go, get a dishclout to make clean your shoes,
and I'll speak for the properties. — My lord, we must
have a shoulder of mutton for our property, and a little
vinegar to make our devil roar.

LORD. Very well. (*To* SERVANTS.) Sirrah, see that they want
nothing.

Dressing up and disrobing

An Elizabethan theatre's wardrobe department was its prime
asset, a priority reflected in the detailed inventory drawn up in
1602 by the actor–manager Edward Alleyn of all the 'Cloaks,
Gowns… Jerkins and Doublets' and other apparel then available in the tiring-house of the new Fortune playhouse (built in
1600, across the river in Clerkenwell, to escape competition
from the Globe). It surfaces, too, in Shakespeare's Sonnet 52,
which glosses the commonplace theme of absence making the
heart grow fonder by likening reunion with his friend to the
sense of dazzling potential on opening a sumptuous wardrobe.

from Sonnet 52 (published 1609):

> So is the time that keeps you as my chest,
> Or as the wardrobe which the robe doth hide,
> To make some special instant special bless'd
> By new unfolding his imprison'd pride.

Shakespeare repeatedly exploited this central spectacle of his
drama, most obviously in the multiple disguisings and gender-
bending (cross-)dressings-up of his Comedies, which seem
from the first to have conveyed the shiver of an unexpected
backstage glimpse, as in *The Two Gentlemen of Verona*, when
Lucetta, a lady's maid (played by a boy), advises Julia, her mistress (played by another), on the best disguise to adopt on her
illicit journey to court to meet her beloved Proteus – and on
the male styles now in fashion.

The Two Gentlemen of Verona (1592), 2.7:

LUCETTA. But in what habit will you go along?

JULIA. Not like a woman, for I would prevent
    The loose encounters of lascivious men.
    Gentle Lucetta, fit me with such °weeds
    As may beseem some well-reputed page.

LUCETTA. Why then, your ladyship must cut your hair.

JULIA. No, girl, I'll knit it up in silken strings
    With twenty odd-conceited true-love knots.
    To be fantastic may become a youth
    Of °greater time than I shall show to be.

LUCETTA. What fashion, madam, shall I make your
    breeches?

JULIA. That fits as well as 'Tell me, good my lord,
    What °compass will you wear your farthingale?'
    Why, e'en what fashion thou best likes, Lucetta.

LUCETTA. You must needs have them with a °codpiece, madam.

JULIA. Out, out, Lucetta! That will be °ill-favour'd.

LUCETTA. A round °hose, madam, now's not worth a pin
    Unless you have a codpiece to stick pins on.

JULIA. Lucetta, as thou lov'st me, let me have
    What thou think'st °meet and is most mannerly.
    But tell me, wench, how will the world repute me
    For undertaking so °unstaid a journey?
    I fear me it will make me scandaliz'd.

A decade or so later, in *Othello*, Shakespeare darkly reversed the bantering intimacy and vulnerability of this exchange. Commanded to prepare for bed by her jealous husband the Moor (in fact her death-bed, as she correctly intuits), Desdemona is helped to undress by Emilia, and the two women reflect on their constricted status ('O, these men! These men!') as the elaborate pins, ties, and knots of her clothing are removed – a fairly lengthy operation given the complexity of contemporary costume. The 'Song of Willow' that Desdemona performs, and which uniquely appears in the play's Folio text, seems to have been designed to accompany the full extent of that action. (Modern-dress productions featuring evening-gowns with zips risk betraying the subtlety of the unfolding scene.)

Othello (1603), 4.3:

DESDEMONA. He says he will return °incontinent,
    And hath commanded me to go to bed,
    And bid me to dismiss you.

EMILIA.   Dismiss me?

DESDEMONA. It was his bidding. Therefore, good Emilia,
    Give me my nightly wearing, and adieu.
    We must not now displease him.

EMILIA. I would you had never seen him.

DESDEMONA. So would not I: my love doth so approve him
    That even his stubbornness, his checks, his frowns —
    Prithee unpin me — have grace and favour.

EMILIA. I have laid those sheets you bade me on the bed.

DESDEMONA. All's one. Good faith, how foolish are our minds!
    If I do die before thee, prithee shroud me
    In one of these same sheets.

EMILIA.   Come, come, you talk!

DESDEMONA. My mother had a maid called Barbary;
    She was in love, and he she lov'd prov'd mad
    And did forsake her. She had a 'Song of Willow' —
    An old thing 'twas, but it express'd her fortune
    And she died singing it. That song tonight
    Will not go from my mind. I have much to do
    But to go hang my head all at one side
    And sing it like poor Barbary. Prithee dispatch.

EMILIA. Shall I go fetch your night-gown?

DESDEMONA.   No, unpin me here.

The extent to which the daily fabric of our lives 'expressed [our] fortune', from christening robe to shroud, via a fool's patchwork motley or a soldier's uniform, coxcomb or crown, repeatedly directed Shakespeare's imagination, and nowhere more subtly than in the Tragedies, where costume itself – or its lack – bears the full burden of a desolate theme. Only think of the weirdly vivid metaphor Angus uses to describe Macbeth, who is said to feel his usurped kingship 'Hang loose about him, like a giant's robe / Upon a dwarfish thief' (5.2). Or the crazed King Lear's confrontation with Edgar, naked and filthy in his guise as the mad beggar Poor Tom: 'Is man no more than this? Consider him well. Thou owest the worm no silk, the beast no hide, the sheep no wool… Off, off, you lendings! Come, unbutton here' (3.4). Or the 'customary suits of solemn black' to which Hamlet contrasts his own, profounder grief:

Hamlet (1600–1), 1.2:

QUEEN. Thou know'st 'tis common: all that lives must die,
    Passing through nature to eternity.

HAMLET. Ay, madam, it is common.

QUEEN.   If it be,
    Why seems it so particular with thee?

HAMLET. 'Seems', madam? Nay, it is. I know not 'seems'.
    'Tis not alone my inky cloak, good mother,
    Nor customary suits of solemn black,
    Nor windy suspiration of forc'd breath,
    No, nor the °fruitful river in the eye,
    Nor the °dejected 'haviour of the visage,
    Together with all forms, moods, shapes of grief,
    That can denote me truly. These indeed 'seem',
    For they are actions that a man might play;
    But I have that within me which passes show,
    These but the trappings and the suits of woe.

Hamlet's 'inky cloak' of mourning, stark against the gaudy costumes of his uncle's court, presents an immediately vivid stage picture of his bitter sense of intellectual and existential isolation.

Shakespeare reversed the tableau in the first scene of *All's Well That Ends Well* (1604), set in a house of mourning, its members 'all in black' (as Shakespeare's own stage-direction specifies), on to which the flashy tinsel of the braggart Parolles's costume jarringly intrudes. 'The soul of this man is his clothes,' warns Lord Lafew later: 'Trust him not in matter of heavy consequence' (2.5).

Elsewhere, the surreptitious plotting of Julius Caesar's assassination is imagined, in a piece of dialogue doubling as a stage-direction, and conjuring a shadowy night on the sunlit stage of its performance, in terms of the decidedly un-Roman hats and cloaks of Elizabethan fashion. So much so, indeed, that Lucius's emblematic description uncannily prefigures the huddled brims and collars of the famous (and entirely fictional) engraved portrait of the Gunpowder Plotters, six years later.

Julius Caesar (1599), 2.1:

BRUTUS.   Do you know them?

LUCIUS. No, sir, their hats are °pluck'd about their ears
    And half their faces buried in their cloaks,
    That by no means I may discover them
    By any °mark of favour.

BRUTUS.   Let 'em enter.

                                        Exit LUCIUS.

They are the faction. O Conspiracy!
Sham'st thou to show thy dangerous brow by night,
When evils are most free? O, then by day
Where wilt thou find a cavern dark enough
To mask thy monstrous visage?

The Swiss tourist Thomas Platter witnessed a production of *Julius Caesar* at the Globe ('the house with the thatched roof') on 21 September 1599. 'The actors are most expensively and elaborately costumed,' he noted in his journal, 'for it is the English custom for eminent lords or knights to bequeath and leave almost the best of their clothes to their serving-men, which it is unseemly for the latter to wear, so that they offer them then for sale for a small sum to the actors.' The hand-me-down nature of an actor's transient finery seems to have preoccupied Shakespeare, even after – indeed, *especially* after – he had secured wealth, fame, and (that symbolic and abstract piece of clothing) a coat-of-arms.

'Appearance and reality', that anaemic cliché of the Eng Lit exam paper, was daily enacted and transfused in the gorgeous spectacle of Shakespeare's theatre: 'Opinion's but a fool,' concludes Simonides in *Pericles* (1608), 'that makes us scan / The outward habit for the inward man' (2.2). But from first to last it was as much the flimsy trash of these baubles as their sumptuous spectacle that informed the world he staged. As when Queen Margaret (she of the 'tiger's heart wrapp'd in a woman's hide': see above, p. 35) viciously taunts the captive pretender to the throne, the Duke of York, by setting a 'paper crown' on his head (a stage effect that works best, of course, when the rest of his costume is gorgeously rich):

Henry VI, Part Three (1592), 1.4:

MARGARET. What, was it you that would be England's king?
    Was't you that revell'd in our parliament
    And made a preachment of your high descent? […]
    Why art thou patient, man? Thou shouldst be mad,
    And I to make thee mad do mock thee thus.
    Stamp, rave, and fret, that I may sing and dance.
    Thou wouldst be fee'd, I see, to make me sport.
    York cannot speak unless he wear a crown. —
    A crown for York, and, lords, bow low to him.
    Hold you his hands whilst I do set it on.

                    She sets a paper crown on his head.

    Ay, marry, sir, now looks he like a king! […]
    Off with the crown, and with the crown, his head;
    And whilst we breathe, take time to do him dead!

Towards the end of his career, Shakespeare modulated the theme into a comic key in the subplot of *The Tempest*, when Caliban's plot to assassinate Prospero, with the aid of a drunkard and a fool, founders on their childish attraction to the vacuous glitter of a wardrobe of fine clothes. It is significant that the word 'frippery', which has come to mean a piece of trivial nonsense, was originally used (as Trinculo uses it here) to mean a stock or store of second-hand or cast-off clothes: the contents, in short, of the Globe's tiring-house. We must imagine Caliban's exasperated question being directed at the audience, and to us.

The Tempest (1612), 4.1:

TRINCULO. O worthy Stephano! Look what a wardrobe here is for thee!

CALIBAN. Let it alone, thou fool, it is but trash.

TRINCULO. O-ho, monster! We know what belongs to a frippery. (*Donning a robe.*) O King Stephano!

STEPHANO. Put off that gown, Trinculo. By this hand, I'll have that gown.

TRINCULO. Thy grace shall have it.

CALIBAN. The °dropsy drown this fool! What do you mean to dote thus on such luggage?

Make-up and beards

When Peter Quince casts the adolescent bellows-mender Francis Flute as Thisbe, his reedy voice pipes up with an objection: 'Nay, faith, let me not play a woman. I have a beard coming.' 'That's all one,' replies Quince, ever unflappable: 'You shall play it in a mask, and you may speak as small [= *high-voiced*] as you will' (1.2). The reference is not to a theatrical mask – of the sort familiar to us from Greek Tragedy, Japanese Noh, or the work of Edward Gordon Craig – but to the fashion among rich Elizabethan women to wear a protective visor against the sun, and so maintain the noble pallor of their complexion. (To be sunburnt, after all, was to resemble a peasant labourer.) The exchange playfully encapsulates two aspects of Shakespeare's stage lost to our modern one: namely, the lead-white complexions of its female characters (played by boys, of course), on the one hand, and the extraordinary degree to which the character of any male role was flagged and determined by the style of his beard.

Ben Jonson stages a lady's stint at her dressing-table ('Methinks 'tis here not white...') in his Roman tragedy *Sejanus* (1603), and Shakespeare has Hamlet focus his misogynist resentment on the 'paintings' of Ophelia's make-up – 'God hath given you one face, and you make yourselves another' (3.1) – which lays the foundation of the bitter joke he cracks when handling Yorick's skull in the graveyard: 'Now get you to my lady's chamber and tell her, let her paint an inch thick, to this favour she must come. Make her laugh at that' (5.1). Altogether more sublime, however, is the use to which Shakespeare puts such backstage cosmetics in *The Winter's Tale*. Believing his innocent wife Hermione dead – killed, he thinks, by the savagery of his own groundless accusations of infidelity – King Leontes is shown her statue by Paulina, evidently a masterpiece of the art. But the 'statue', realistically painted as all such pieces then were, is, of course, Hermione herself – white of face, and 'rubious' of lip. A familiar domestic moment between man and wife ('Don't kiss, you'll smudge me!'), albeit mediated here by Paulina, is transfigured into a meditation on the related potential of theatrical art and spiritual resurrection.

The Winter's Tale (1610), 5.3:

LEONTES.   Still methinks
　There is an air comes from her. What fine chisel
　Could ever yet cut breath? Let no man mock me,
　For I will kiss her.

PAULINA.   Good my lord, forbear:
　The ruddiness upon her lip is wet;
　You'll mar it if you kiss it, stain your own
　With oily painting. Shall I draw the curtain?

LEONTES. No, not these twenty years. [...]
　　　　　　　　　　　　O, she's warm!

If this be magic, let it be an art
Lawful as eating.

POLIXENES.   She embraces him!

CAMILLO. She hangs about his neck —
If she pertain to life, let her speak too!

'Neither will I meddle with our variety of beards,' wrote William Harrison in his 1586 *Description of England*, steering away from the evidently controversial topic that was squarely addressed by Philip Stubbes in his extended Puritan grumble about London's 'Abuses': 'One a gentleman's cut, another the common cut, one cut of the court, another of the country, with infinite the like varieties which I do overpass… When you come to be trimmed, they will ask you whether you will be cut to look terrible to your enemy, or amiable to your friend, grim or stern in countenance, or pleasant and demure'. This 'infinite variety' of male self-presentation supplied an extra dimension to the resources of the Elizabethan tiring-house, with a range of artificial beards recognizably appropriate to the parts they furnished – as witness the different styles sported by the soldier and the justice in Jaques's 'Seven Ages of Man' speech (see above, p. 42). When Gower, the English captain in *Henry V*, deplores the braggart Pistol's imposture as a war veteran (which was a true scandal of London life at the time), he may as well be describing an actor's performance, from his learning 'by rote' of his part, via the appropriate improvisation of some 'new-tuned oaths', and the well-worn uniform of his costume – to the 'beard of the General's cut' that he sports.

Henry V (1599), 3.6:

GOWER. Why, 'tis a gull, a fool, a rogue, that now and then
goes to the wars, to grace himself at his return into
London under the form of a soldier. And such fellows
are perfect in the great commanders' names, and they
will learn you by rote where services were done — at
such and such a °sconce, at such a breach, at such a
convoy; who came off bravely, who was shot, who

disgraced, what terms the enemy stood on. And this
they con perfectly in the °phrase of war, which they
trick up with new-tuned oaths. And what a beard of
the General's cut and a °horrid suit of the camp will do
among foaming bottles and ale-washed wits, is
wonderful to be thought on.

'The General' was the Earl of Essex, the cut of whose broad,
spade-like beard was as famous in the sixteenth century as a
Zapata, Kitchener, or Clark Gable moustache was in the twentieth, and accordingly imitated for real. (The Earl, whose
farcically abortive *coup d'état* led to his execution a couple of
years later, was a charismatic mixture of all three.) That particular style – along with many others – seems to have been
available from an off-the-peg section of the Globe's tiring-
house. Surviving inventories from 1550 ('iiij beards of coney
skins & white fur & fox') and 1605 ('3 beards one Red one
black th'other flaxen') certainly detail numerous styles and
colours of beard – though Bottom's scrupulous connoisseur-
ship, like a would-be Orson Welles with a box of false noses,
is of course intended as absurd.

A Midsummer Night's Dream (1595), 1.2:

QUINCE. Therefore you must needs play Pyramus.

BOTTOM. Well, I will undertake it. What beard were I best
to play it in?

QUINCE. Why, what you will.

BOTTOM. I will discharge it in either your straw-colour
beard — your orange-tawny beard — your purple-in-
grain beard — or your French-crown-colour beard,
your perfect yellow.

QUINCE. Some of your French crowns have no hair at all,
and then you will play bare-faced!

'Vile and raggèd foils'

When Ben Jonson revised his earliest surviving play, *Every Man in His Humour* (1598), he relocated its action from Florence to London, anglicized all the characters' names, and supplied a new Prologue (below) that poked fun at the 'ill customs' of an earlier theatrical tradition. For all that *Henry V* may have dazzlingly advertised the resources of the brand-new Globe, the genre of the History play was beginning to show its age: this was Shakespeare's ninth or tenth, and writers were running out of kings and queens to write about. Jonson had himself written a historical tragedy – now lost – about Richard III, but he found his métier in a new style of comical satire that eschewed (as his Prologue details) such clichés of rival forms.

Not for Jonson the protracted business of chronicle history, by which a protagonist ages sixty years in an afternoon or two, 'in one beard and weed [= *garment*]', and by the judicious backstage application of make-up (if this is not merely a metaphor) to transform 'wounds to scars': his play observes the Classical unities of time and place, its action taking place within a single city and the working hours of a single day. Depending on when he wrote it, Jonson may also have had in his sights the Chorus of Time in *The Winter's Tale* (1610), who blithely announces the passage of sixteen years between Acts Two and Three, and the instantaneous growth from 'swaddled' baby to beautiful princess of its young heroine, Perdita. The swipes at Shakespeare's earlier Chorus, in *Henry V*, are more easily identified – in the demotion of the 'four or five most vile and raggèd foils' for which the former so eloquently apologizes, for example, to a set of 'three rusty swords' and some swanky words, or in the airy navigation it demands of its audience ('wafts you o'er the seas'). Jonson's enjoyable survey of these (sometimes literally) 'creaking' effects affords a rare glimpse of the various duties of the Elizabethan ASM.

There is the 'throne' by which the pagan gods seem routinely to have descended through the wooden canopy over the stage – the so-called 'heavens' – as a *deus ex machina*: Henslowe paid the considerable sum of £7 'for carpenters' work & making the throne in the heavens' of the Rose in the mid-1590s, and Shakespeare made more work for carpenters and model-makers as late as 1610 when, towards the end of *Cymbeline*, '*Jupiter descends in thunder and lightning, sitting upon an eagle: he throws a thunderbolt*' (5.4). Such effects must have demanded more than their fair share of an audience's 'imaginary forces' to be taken seriously (Jonson's sardonic reference to the pleasure they induced in 'boys' presumably refers to the immature giggling familiar still from matinees of GCSE-set plays). Nor does the spoilsport Jonson refrain from pulling back the curtain on such Wizardry of Oz. Thunder and lightning? Merely a hefty cannon-ball dropped and rolled on the backstage floorboards, to the accompaniment of a kettle-drum. A 'thunderbolt'? Only the 'nimble squib' of a firecracker – carefully aimed (usually) in these thatched premises, and just enough to give the ladies a fright. (Unlike its modern replica, Shakespeare's original Globe was neither furnished with a sprinkler system nor required to announce its productions' inclusion of 'sudden loud noises'.)

from Ben Jonson, Prologue to *Every Man in His Humour* (published 1616)

PROLOGUE. Though need make many poets, and some such
    As Art and Nature have not better'd much,
    Yet ours, for want, hath not so lov'd the stage
    As he dare serve th'ill customs of the age,
    Or purchase your delight at such a rate
    As, for it, he himself must justly hate.
    To make a child, now swaddled, to proceed
    Man, and then shoot up, in one beard and weed,
    Past three-score years; or, with three rusty swords
    And help of some few foot-and-half-foot words
    Fight over York and Lancaster's long jars;
    And in the tiring-house bring wounds to scars.
    He rather prays you will be pleas'd to see
    One such today as other plays should be —
    Where neither Chorus wafts you o'er the seas;
    Nor creaking throne comes down, the boys to please;
    Nor nimble squib is seen, to make afear'd

The gentlewomen; nor roll'd bullet heard,
To say it thunders; nor tempestuous drum
Rumbles, to tell you when the storm doth come:
But deeds, and language, such as men do use,
And persons such as Comedy would choose
When she would show an image of the times
And sport with human follies, not with crimes.

Two tricks of the trade

If replicas of food were routinely stored in the props basket backstage, so real foodstuffs seem elsewhere to have helped along the stage illusion – whether in the judicious dab of an onion to prompt the tears appropriate to a tragic recitation, or the Elizabethan equivalent of 'Kensington gore', in the form of a 'bladder' of red-wine vinegar concealed beneath an actor's shirt.

The Taming of the Shrew (1592), Induction, Scene 1:

LORD. And if the boy have not a woman's gift
    To rain a shower of commanded tears,
    An onion will do well for such a shift,
    Which in a napkin being close convey'd
    Shall in despite enforce a watery eye.
    See this dispatch'd with all the haste thou canst:
    Anon I'll give thee more instructions.

from Thomas Preston, *Cambyses* (1570):

SMIRDIS. Yet pardon me, I heartily you pray!
    Consider: the King is a tyrant tyrannious
    And all his doings be damnable and pernicious.
    Favour me therefore — I did never him offend.

CRUELTY. No favour at all. Your life is at an end.
    Even now I strike, his body to wound!

                            Strike him in divers places.

Behold: now his blood springs out on the ground!
A little bladder of vinegar pricked.

On second thoughts…

The draft scripts Shakespeare delivered to his company at least twice a year for nearly twenty years supplied the raw material for a succession of popular productions that have inexhaustibly lasted the four centuries since. But as modern scholarship has scrupulously ascertained, the printed texts of many of these plays – the necessary basis of our knowledge of them – differ, often substantially, from their original drafts. Changes and emendations to that first batch of script came about for a variety of reasons, many of them familiar to modern dramatists, and many of which are enjoyably caricatured in poor Peter Quince's rehearsals for *Pyramus and Thisbe* (below). In advance of such group rehearsals, for example, and as we have seen, any improvised sequences would be assigned to the company Clown to 'work up', and these routines would later be introduced to the 'book' of the working script. The timorous silence Snug maintains for the duration of the scene does not augur particularly well for his extemporized roaring as the Lion – though the argument that breaks out over his head about it keenly reflects the concerns of Shakespeare's own company.

Quince has already warned against the Lion being *too* realistic, for fear it should scare the female members of the audience and so 'hang us all' (1.2; see above, p. 63). While the Lord Chamberlain's Men never precisely risked capital punishment for the realism of their performance, their staging of *Richard II* at the Globe in February 1601, on the eve of the Essex rebellion, and at the conspirators' request, came shiveringly close to doing so. (One of the company shareholders, the actor Augustine Phillips, gave evidence at Essex's capital trial. His explanation – that the company had been offered £2 to stage such an old play, so 'long out of use' – was accepted by the court.) Playwrights and actors alike meanwhile routinely endured periods of imprisonment for political impertinence – Jonson in 1597 for a scandalous satire he wrote with Thomas Nashe (who fled to Norfolk, never to return); and Jonson again (along with co-authors Marston and Chapman) for disobliging references to the Scots in *Eastward Ho!* (1605). In both these cases, it was the players' failure to submit the material to the Master of Revels in advance of performance that prompted such retribution. 'Leave out ye insurrection wholly,' reads that state censor's marginal note in the manuscript of a draft play about Sir Thomas More to which Shakespeare himself is thought to have contributed. The cautious objections and collective discussion we overhear among the amateur mechanicals, fearful of offending their powerful audience, had a basis in hard fact.

A Midsummer Night's Dream (1595), 3.1:

BOTTOM. Peter Quince?

PETER. What saist thou, °bully Bottom?

BOTTOM. There are things in this Comedy of Pyramus and Thisbe that will never please. First, Pyramus must draw a sword to kill himself — which the ladies cannot abide. How answer you that?

SNOUT. °By'r la'kin, a °parlous fear!

STARVELING. I believe we must leave the killing out, when all is done.

BOTTOM. Not a whit! I have a device to make all well. Write me a Prologue, and let the Prologue seem to say, 'We will do no harm with our swords,' and that Pyramus is not killed indeed. And for the more better assurance, tell them that I, Pyramus, am not Pyramus but Bottom the weaver: this will put them out of fear.

QUINCE. Well, we will have such a Prologue, and it shall be written in °eight-and-six.

BOTTOM. No, make it two more, let it be written in eight-and-eight.

SNOUT. Will not the ladies be afraid of the lion?

STARVELING. I fear it, I promise you.

BOTTOM. Masters, you ought to consider with yourself:
to bring in (God shield us!) a lion among ladies is a
most dreadful thing. For there is not a more fearful
°wildfowl than your lion living — and we ought to
look to it.

SNOUT. Therefore another Prologue must tell he is not a
lion.

BOTTOM. Nay, you must name his name, and half his face
must be seen through the lion's neck, and he himself
must speak through, saying thus (or to the same
°defect): 'Ladies' — or 'Fair ladies, I would wish you'
— or 'I would request you' — or 'I would entreat you
not to fear — not to tremble. My life for yours. If you
think I come hither as a lion, it were pity of my life.
No, I am no such thing: I am a man, as other men are
—' and there indeed let him name his name, and tell
them plainly he is Snug the joiner.

QUINCE. Well, it shall be so. But there is two hard things:
that is, to bring the moonlight into a chamber — for
you know, Pyramus and Thisbe meet by moonlight.

SNOUT. Doth the moon shine that night we play our play?

BOTTOM. A calendar, a calendar! Look in the almanac,
find out moonshine, find out moonshine.

QUINCE. Yes, it doth shine that night.

BOTTOM. Why then may you leave a °casement of the
great chamber window (where we play) open, and the
moon may shine in at the casement.

QUINCE. Ay; or else one must come in with a bush of
thorns and a lantern, and say he comes to °disfigure, or
to present, the person of Moonshine. Then there is
another thing: we must have a wall in the great
chamber, for Pyramus and Thisbe (says the story) did
talk through the chink of a wall.

SNOUT. You can never bring in a wall. — What say you,
   Bottom?

BOTTOM. Some man or other must present Wall — and
   let him have some plaster, or some °loam, or some
   rough-cast about him, to signify Wall; or let him hold
   his fingers thus, and through that cranny shall
   Pyramus and Thisbe whisper.

QUINCE. If that may be, then all is well. Come, sit down,
   °every mother's son, and rehearse your parts. Pyramus,
   you begin; when you have spoken your speech, enter
   into that °brake, and so every one according to his cue.

'O do not swear...'

Starveling's proposal to 'leave the killing out' entirely for fear
of giving offence remains impressively oblivious to the fun-
damental premise of the play they are rehearsing. But while
such extreme revisions are manifestly absurd, authoritarian
jurisdiction over Shakespeare's stage often resulted in equally
ridiculous effects. The author of *Richard II*, for example, must
surely have been nonplussed to see its Quarto paperback sell
out through three editions (1597–8), despite omitting its central scene (in which Richard II yields his crown to the
charismatic Henry IV). Although evidently *performed* (danger-
ously, as we have seen, in 1601), that contentious sequence
was not allowed to appear *in print* until after King James I's
smooth accession to the throne in 1603 – but the new reign
swiftly brought new constraints. Among the consequences of
the king's apparently miraculous survival of the Gunpowder
Plot in November 1605 was the newly emphatic piety
imposed by Act of Parliament on plays and players in the following year.

from 'An Act to Restrain Abuses of Players' (27 May 1606):

> For the preventing and avoiding of the great Abuse of the Holy Name of God [...] Be it enacted [...] that if at any time or times [...] any person or persons do or shall in any Stage Play, Interlude, Show, May-game, or Pageant jestingly or profanely speak or use the Holy Name of God, or of Christ Jesus, or of the Holy Ghost, or of the Trinity, which are not to be spoken but with fear and reverence, shall forfeit for every such offence by him or them committed Ten Pounds.

The edict retrospectively applied to the performance of old plays as well as to the writing of new ones – which is why some of its effects remain visible in the differences between Elizabethan Quarto and Jacobean Folio texts of some of Shakespeare's plays, where the latter have been set from scripts doctored by the company to comply with the 1606 legislation. Similar revisions still today routinely accompany a new stage-play's adaptation from the foul-mouthed stage to the more decorous confines of a BBC Radio production: the 'reform nun' who 'drops her knickers' mentioned in the Radio 3 production of Tom Stoppard's *Rock 'n' Roll* (2007), for example, gave more intimate favours in the play's original Royal Court production and published script (2006). Among the more damaging examples from Shakespeare's day must be counted the loss of one of Richard of Gloucester's better jokes – namely his own pretended affront at Buckingham's use of the mild expletive 'Zounds' (a conflation of 'God's wounds').

Richard III (uncensored 1597 Quarto text), 3.7:

BUCKINGHAM. And in this resolution here we leave you.
　　Come, citizens. Zounds, I'll entreat no more!

RICHARD. O do not swear, my Lord of Buckingham.

　　　　　　Exeunt BUCKINGHAM, MAYOR, *and* CITIZENS.

CATESBY. Call them again, my lord; accept their suit.

Richard III (censored 1623 Folio text), 3.7:

BUCKINGHAM. And in this resolution here we leave you.
  Come, citizens. We will entreat no more.

> *Exeunt* BUCKINGHAM, MAYOR, *and* CITIZENS.

CATESBY. Call him again, sweet Prince; accept their suit.

Shakespeare's reference, in his Sonnet 66, to an 'art made tongue-tied by authority' combines his keen sense of an actor's nerves (see below, p. 132) with the frustration of a writer whose art was severely patrolled by the state. The 'device' that Bottom comes up with to forestall any possible offence when his character kills himself ('Write me a Prologue, and let the Prologue seem to say... that Pyramus is not killed indeed') – and Snout's suggestion of yet 'another Prologue' to explain that the play's Lion is not a real lion – drolly exaggerates both the permanent deference of Shakespeare's own 'mechnical' trade as a playwright, and the means by which his theatre company so often tailored their plays to the specific circumstances of its première, transfer, or revival.

We have seen how Shakespeare's Chorus to *Henry V* may have commanded his first audience's attention to the auspices of the new Globe, and how Jonson supplemented his thoroughly revised comedy with a new Prologue for its revival. Henslowe confirms a common practice when he records the payment of five shillings to Thomas Middleton 'for a prologue & A epilogue for the play of [Greene's *Friar*] *Bacon* for the court' in December 1602, while the ageing Thomas Heywood supplied two prologues, to be 'spoken at Court' and 'to the Stage, at the Cockpit', and an epilogue, for a revival of Marlowe's *Jew of Malta* in the 1630s – fully forty years or so after its première. Brainstorming a suitable prologue for such a transfer was part and parcel of a jobbing playwright's career – as John Marston rather deliciously shows in his depiction of another touring company's rehearsals in *Histriomastix* (printed 1610). This time, however, the problem isn't an over-bumptious leading actor, but an overly pretentious principal dramatist whose new Prologue seems to expect its audience to imaginatively see the horses to which it refers, piecing out the players' imperfections with their thoughts. 'Bayard' was a slang term for an old blind nag, compared to Alexander the Great's legendarily agile mount by the fluently creative Master Posthaste. (Who *can* Marston have been thinking of?)

John Marston, *Histriomastix* (1599–1600), 4.3:

Enter [the PLAYERS, *severally].*

GULCH. °Jack of the clock-house, where's Master Posthaste?

BELCH. In my book for Slowpace – twelve-pence on's pate for staying so late!

GULCH. Gut! Prologue, begin! Rehearse.

GUT. 'Gentlemen, in this envious age we bring
Bayard for Bucephalus: if mirèd, bogg'd,
Draw him forth with your favours.
So, promising that we never mean to perform,
Our Prologue pieceth —'

GULCH. 'Pieceth'? What peaking pageanter penned that?

BELCH. Who but Master Posthaste?

GULCH. It is as dangerous to read his name at a play-door as a printed bill on a plague-door!

Sometimes a play's transfer, or later revival, involved a more substantial revision than the mere topping and tailing of a new Chorus. Henslowe's Diary records payments for 'additions' both to Marlowe's *Doctor Faustus*, and to Kyd's *Spanish Tragedy*, in 1601–2 – presumably for the plays' revival at the new Fortune playhouse, with Edward Alleyn, coaxed from retirement, in the lead roles he had made his own a decade earlier. Ben Jonson was one of those makeshift revisers, and one of the qualities he later praised in Shakespeare was the latter's workmanlike ability to 'sweat… and strike the second heat / Upon the Muse's anvil'. Jonson was an obsessive reviser of his own work (as witness his London version of *Every Man in His Humour* – and his entire rewriting of his collaborator Chapman's scenes for the published text of *Sejanus* in 1605); Shakespeare's skills as a reviser of his own plays were less rigorous (in part because, unlike Jonson, he seems to have displayed little interest in overseeing their publication). It is now generally accepted, however, that the Quarto and Folio versions of *King Lear* present first and second drafts of that masterpiece, via a brilliant 'second heat' of creative work; and that the three surviving texts of *Hamlet* represent complicatedly different stages in that play's theatrical life. All three of those versions include the detail of Hamlet's supplying to the Players a speech of his own, of 'some dozen or sixteen lines', to be inserted into *The Murder of Gonzago* – presumably to finesse his bait for the play he later renames *The Mousetrap*. A lot of scholarly ink has been spilt in efforts to identify that speech in the play-within-the-play we witness; presumably in vain, since the performance we get to see of it is abruptly abandoned midway through.

Hamlet (1600–1), 2.2:

HAMLET. I'll have thee speak out the rest of this soon. — Good my lord, will you see the players well °bestowed? Do you hear? Let them be well used, for they are the °abstract and brief chronicles of the time. After your death you were better have a bad epitaph than their ill report while you live.

POLONIUS. My lord, I will use them according to their desert.

HAMLET. God's bodykins, man, much better. Use every man after his desert and who shall scape whipping? Use them after your own honour and dignity: the less they deserve, the more merit is in your bounty. Take them in.

POLONIUS. Come, sirs.

HAMLET. Follow him, friends. We'll hear a play tomorrow. (*Aside to the* FIRST PLAYER.) Dost thou hear me, old friend? Can you play *The Murder of Gonzago*?

1 PLAYER. Ay, my lord.

HAMLET. We'll ha't tomorrow night. You could, for a need, study a speech of some dozen or sixteen lines, which I would set down and insert in't, could you not?

1 PLAYER. Ay, my lord.

HAMLET. Very well. — Follow that lord, and look you mock him not.

Beginners

The First Player seems unfazed by Hamlet's request, suggesting that such last-minute additions (or cuts) were as routinely supplied to old plays as their catchy alternative titles. Despite *Twelfth Night*, or *What You Will*, and *All Is True*, or *Henry VIII*, it is Thomas Middleton who cornered the market in such (re-)packaging, as in the complex title of his 1611 play, *No {Wit Help} like a Woman's. Or, The Almanac* – but the practice was common. The Index of Plays in R.A. Foakes's definitive edition of *Henslowe's Diary*, for example, includes an entry that reads: '*Bad May Amend* (? the same as *Worse Afeared than Hurt* or *Hannibal and Hermes*)'. The fluidity of a play's title reflected the constantly evolving status of its text, whereby the odd extra speech like Hamlet's competed for space in an actor's memory with the anxious bustle of props, costume, and cues in the hours and minutes before (what we now call) 'curtain-up'. The chaotic storm before the decorous lull of a play's first line is nicely caught both in the 'noises off' supplied by Richard Brome, and in Bottom's final 'notes' and pep-talk.

Richard Brome, *The Antipodes* (1638), 2.1:

LETOY. Go fetch 'em then, while I prepare my actors. Within there, ho!

1 PLAYER (*within*).   This is my beard and hair.

2 PLAYER (*within*). My lord appointed it for my part.

3 PLAYER (*within*).   No.
   This is for you; and this is yours, this grey one.

4 PLAYER (*within*). Where be the °foils and targets for the
      women?

1 PLAYER (*within*). Here, can't you see?

LETOY.   What a °rude coil is there!
   But yet it pleases me.

1 PLAYER (*within*).   You must not wear
   That cloak and hat.

2 PLAYER (*within*).   Who told you so? I must,
   In my first scene, and you must wear that robe.

LETOY. What a noise make those knaves!

A Midsummer Night's Dream (1595), 4.2:

BOTTOM. Get your apparel together, good strings to your
   beards, new ribbons to your pumps. Meet presently at
   the palace; every man look o'er his part. For the short
   and the long is, our play is preferred! In any case, let
   Thisbe have clean linen; and let not him that plays the
   lion pare his nails, for they shall hang out for the lion's
   claws. And, most dear actors, eat no onions nor garlic,
   for we are to utter sweet breath, and I do not doubt but
   to hear them say it is a sweet comedy. No more words
   — away! Go, away!

Interlude

A 'Finished' Script

A work is never finished, always abandoned.

Paul Valéry (1921)

'This text went to press before the end of rehearsals,' reads a modern playwright's Author's Note, 'and so may differ slightly from the play as performed.' Much the same sort of standard disclaimer – or, rather, a wide range of more substantial editorial explanations – should properly preface all the surviving texts of Shakespeare's plays and those of his contemporaries. The publication of a new play is nowadays usually timetabled to coincide with its première, resulting in a prematurely 'definitive' version, which its second edition sometimes corrects. In Shakespeare's time, however, a play's publication was always a secondary consideration, not least since it threatened the company's monopoly over its production, and it was usually at least three or four years before a successful play appeared in print – if it did so at all. When Shakespeare's fellow actors John Heminge and Henry Condell compiled a Collected Edition of his plays in 1623 (the First Folio), around half were being published for the first time; and though over 400 plays survive from the period 1567–1642, as many again and more are known to have been produced. Nor did a play's published text ever reliably reflect 'the play as performed'. At one end of the scale are the scrappy, probably illicit Quarto editions, patched together from the faulty memory of a handful of its original cast, and 'pirated' (or bootlegged) on the open market, which at best supply a foggy impression of its original

run. At the other lies the claim, by the publisher of the Beau-
mont and Fletcher Folio Works (1647), to present 'All that was
acted, and all that was not' (since 'some scenes and passages'
were routinely omitted in production). In between sits the
bewildering range of sheer chance responsible for the versions
of those plays that have come down to us.

True, none of these so-called 'textual transmissions' was
affected by their principal actor being transformed into a donkey by a malicious goblin, but Peter Quince's appalled reaction
is nevertheless revealing: 'Bless thee, Bottom, bless thee! Thou
art translated!' And it is a paper-chase string of such 'translations'
that extends beyond all the neat paperback editions to which we
have such easy access today. The sole surviving original text of
Macbeth, for example, is that of an adaptation made by Thomas
Middleton for a revival performed a decade or so after its première, probably without Shakespeare's knowledge. *King Lear*
and *Othello* exist in two distinct versions, *Hamlet* in three – each
of them differently 'authentic' – and the unique Folio text of *All's
Well That Ends Well* seems never to have been performed as such
in Shakespeare's lifetime. And while the Quarto of Shakespeare's late collaborative smash-hit *Pericles* was printed so badly
that editors since Heminge and Condell themselves have wished
it would go away, every single line of his *Love's Labours Won* (a
play praised in 1598 and known to have been printed by 1603)
has disappeared – along with the original script of *Cardenio*
(1614), another of his collaborations with Fletcher, which may
exist, like a disturbed archaeological layer, somewhere deep
beneath the surface of an eighteenth-century adaptation.

Furthermore, even when it is known (which it often isn't)
from what exactly it was that a published edition was set into
type (an author's first draft? a company prompt-book? a
memorial reconstruction? an annotated previous edition? a
revised adaptation by someone else?), the sheer notion of an
author's definitive wording risks disappearing among a jostling
chorus of actors, adapters, directors, copyists, typesetters,
proof-readers, editors, scholars, and – in the case of Peter
Quince's *Pyramus and Thisbe* – audiences. As a playful illustration of this process, the following section presents an edited

text of Quince's play, reconstructed like a jigsaw puzzle from the glimpses afforded of its rehearsal and performance throughout *A Midsummer Night's Dream*. I found this a surprisingly difficult task, and readers must feel welcome to disagree with my decisions – in which case they may perhaps piece out their understanding of the far larger decisions guiding all modern play-texts derived from the Shakespearean stage.

The close source for Peter Quince's re-telling of the story of Pyramus and Thisbe is Ovid's *Metamorphoses*, in Arthur Golding's 1567 translation – such a favourite in Shakespeare's own library that he brought it onstage as a prop in his *Titus Andronicus* (1592). Indeed, one of the subtler jokes in the sublime comedy of the mechanicals' rehearsal and performance is Duke Theseus's peremptory dismissal of Quince's Epilogue (see below, p. 180). Rather as King Claudius brings down the curtain on *The Murder of Gonzago; or, The Mousetrap* before we have the chance to identify the 'dozen or sixteen lines' that Hamlet himself has supplied, so we never hear the entire point of Ovid's fable: the transformation (or metamorphosis) of the 'unhappy tree' where the lovers die. Originally 'a fair high mulberry with fruit as white as snow', following the copious bloodshed that ensues (worthy of Tarantino), its berries miraculously turned a 'deep dark purple colour', as they 'mourning-like' remain to this day – 'For when the fruit is throughly ripe, the berry is bespeck'd / With colour tending to a black'. (Much the same metamorphosis attends the climax to Shakespeare's long poem *Venus and Adonis* from a year or two before, where a 'purple flower… chequer'd with white' springs up from the dead Adonis's blood.)* Scholars usually explain Peter Quince's surname by reference to its pun, appropriate to his day-job as a carpenter, on the wooden wedges known as 'quines' or 'quoins' – in the same way that Snug's name makes a snug fit with his occupation as a joiner. The fact that the fruitily named Quince's Classical fable of another fruit-tree never in fact comes to fruition, however, may be another joke.

---

* This may explain why Oberon's account of the colouring of the plant known as 'love-in-idleness' ('purple with love's wound') is apparently Shakespeare's own invention (2.1).

One aspect that emerges most forcefully from my attempted reconstruction is the affectionate comedy by which its players' anxious reluctance not to offend their audience – 'That would hang us, every mother's son' – deliciously results in a play entirely drained of all dramatic tension by its obsessive use of Chorus and Dumb Show. Which, all things considered, is a pretty sophisticated joke from a playwright who had only the previous year deployed an all-but identical plot – two lovers commit suicide following a tragic misunderstanding brought about by their parents' disapproval – in *The Most Excellent and Lamentable Tragedy of Romeo and Juliet*, before apparently abandoning his own planned system of Choruses as he wrote.

THE
MOST LAMENTABLE
Comedy and Most Cruel Death
of

Pyramus and Thisbe:

An Interlude

by Peter Quince

Chorus.	*Peter Quince the carpenter*
Pyramus.	*Nick Bottom the weaver*
Thisbe.	*Francis Flute the bellows-mender*
A Wall.	*Tom Snout the tinker*
Moonshine.	*Robin Starveling the tailor*
A Lion.	*Master Snug the joiner*

Scene 1

Enter CHORUS.

CHORUS. If we offend, it is with our good will
    That you should think we come: not to offend,
    But with good will to show our simple skill.
    That is the true beginning of our °end.
    Consider then, we come (but in °despite
    We do not come) as minding to content you.
    Our true intent is all for your delight —
    We are not here that you should here repent you.
    The actors are at hand, and by their show
    You shall know all that you are like to know.

Exit.

Scene 2

Trumpets.

Enter PYRAMUS *and* THISBE, WALL, MOONSHINE, *and* LION, *for the Dumb Show:* [PYRAMUS *approaches the* WALL, *calls out for* THISBE, *and retires;* THISBE *approaches the* WALL, *calls for* PYRAMUS, *who returns. The lovers whisper through a chink, and exit.* THISBE *enters by* MOONLIGHT, *but drops her cloak when a* LION *scares her away, who mauls it with his bloody mouth.* PYRAMUS *enters, sees the blood-stained cloak, and kills himself in despair. Then* THISBE *enters, sees* PYRAMUS's *body, and kills herself in despair.*]

Enter CHORUS *again.*

CHORUS. Gentles, perchance you wonder at this show,
But wonder on till truth make all things plain.
This man is Pyramus, if you would know;
This beauteous lady Thisbe is, certain;
This man, with °lime and rough-cast, doth present
Wall — that vile wall which did these lovers sunder.
And through Wall's chink, poor souls, they are content
To whisper: at the which, let no man wonder.
This man, with lantern, dog, and bush of thorn,
Presenteth Moonshine. For if you will know,
By moonshine did these lovers think no scorn
To meet at °Ninus' tomb, there, there to woo.
This grizzly beast (which Lion hight by name)
The trusty Thisbe, coming first by night,
Did scare away, or rather did affright;
And as she fled, her mantle she did fall,
Which Lion vile with bloody mouth did stain.
Anon comes Pyramus, sweet youth and tall,
And finds his trusty Thisbe's mantle slain;
Whereat with blade, with bloody blameful blade,
He bravely broach'd his boiling bloody breast,
And Thisbe, tarrying in mulberry shade,
His dagger drew, and died. For all the rest,

Let Lion, Moonshine, Wall, and lovers twain
At large discourse while here they do remain.

Exeunt all but WALL.

WALL. In this same Interlude it doth befall
    That I, one Snout by name, present a wall:
    And such a wall as I would have you think
    That had in it a crannied hole, or chink,
    Through which the lovers, Pyramus and Thisbe,
    Did whisper often, very secretly.
    This loam, this rough-cast, and this stone doth show
    That I am that same wall (the truth is so),
    And this the cranny is, right and °sinìster,
    Through which the fearful lovers are to whisper.

Enter PYRAMUS *on one side. He draws near* WALL.

PYRAMUS. O grim-look'd night, O night with hue so black,
    O night, which ever art when day is not,
    O night, O night, alack, alack, alack,
    I fear my Thisbe's promise is forgot!
    And thou, O wall, thou sweet and lovely wall,
    That stands between her father's ground and mine,
    Thou wall, O wall, O sweet and lovely wall,
    Show me thy chink to blink through with mine eyne.
    Thanks, courteous wall, °Jove shield thee well for this!

He peers through the chink.

But what see I? No Thisbe do I see!
O wicked wall, through whom I see no bliss,
Curs'd be thy stones for thus deceiving me! —
Thisbe! The flowers of odours savours sweet:
So hath thy breath, my dearest Thisbe dear —
But hark, a voice! Stay thou but here a while,
And by and by I will to thee appear.

Exit.

Enter THISBE *on the other side. She draws near* WALL.

THISBE. O wall, full often hast thou heard my moans
   For parting my fair Pyramus and me.
   My cherry lips have often kiss'd thy stones,
   Thy stones with lime and hair knit up in thee.
   Most radiant Pyramus, most lily-white of hue,
   Of colour like the red rose on triumphant briar!
   Most °brisky juvenile, and °eke most lovely °jew,
   As true as truest horse that yet would never tire!

   Enter PYRAMUS.

PYRAMUS. If I were, fair Thisbe, I were only thine.
   (*Aside.*) I see a voice! Now will I to the chink
   To spy °an I can hear my Thisbe's face.
   (*Calls.*) Thisbe?

THISBE.   My love! Thou art my love, I think?

PYRAMUS. Think what thou wilt, I am thy lover's grace,
   And like °Leander am I trusty still.

THISBE. And I like Hero, till the °Fates me kill.

PYRAMUS. Not °Cephalus to Procris was so true.

THISBE. As Cephalus to Procris, I to you.

PYRAMUS. O kiss me through the hole of this vile wall.

THISBE. I kiss the wall's hole, not your lips at all.

PYRAMUS. Wilt thou at Ninus' tomb meet me straightway?

THISBE. I'll meet thee, Pyramus, at Ninus' tomb.
   Most fair Pyramus!
   Tide life, tide death, I come without delay!

                    Exeunt PYRAMUS *and* THISBE.

WALL. Thus have I, Wall, my part dischargèd so:
   And being done, thus Wall away doth go.

                                      Exit.

Scene 3

Enter LION *and* MOONSHINE.

LION. You, ladies, you whose gentle hearts do fear
    The smallest monstrous mouse that creeps on floor,
    May now perchance both quake and tremble here
    When Lion rough in wildest rage doth roar.
    Then know that I as Snug the joiner am
    A lion fell, nor else no lion's dam:
    For if I should as Lion come in strife
    Into this place, 'twere pity of my life.

MOONSHINE. This lantern doth the hornèd moon present;
    Myself the man i' th' moon doth seem to be —
    This thorn-bush my thorn-bush, and this dog my dog.

    Enter THISBE.

THISBE. This is old Ninus' tomb. Where is my love?

LION (*roars*). Ooarh!

    THISBE *drops her cloak, and runs off.*

    The LION *mauls the cloak with his bloody jaws.*

                    Exit LION.

    Enter PYRAMUS.

PYRAMUS. Sweet moon, I thank thee for thy sunny beams;
    I thank thee, moon, for shining now so bright:
    For by thy gracious, golden, glittering gleams,
    I trust to take of truest Thisbe sight —

    He sees the cloak.

    But stay! O spite!
    But mark, poor knight,
    What dreadful dole is here?
    Eyes, do you see?
    How can it be?
    O dainty duck, O dear!
    Thy mantle good —

What, stain'd with blood?
Approach, you Furies fell!
O °Fates, come, come,
Cut °thread and thrum,
°Quail, crush, conclude, and quell!
O wherefore, Nature, didst thou lions frame,
Since lion vile hath here deflower'd my dear,
Which is — no! no! which was — the fairest dame
That liv'd, that lov'd, that lik'd, that look'd with cheer?
Come, tears, confound:
Out sword, and wound
The °pap of Pyramus.
Ay, that left pap
Where heart doth hop.
Thus die I — thus, thus, thus!

He stabs himself.

Now am I dead,
Now am I fled,
My soul is in the sky.
Tongue, lose thy light;
Moon, take thy flight.

Exit MOONSHINE.

Now die, die, die, die, die!

He dies.

Enter THISBE. *She sees* PYRAMUS*'s body.*

THISBE. Asleep, my love? —
What, *dead*, my dove?
O Pyramus arise!
Speak, speak! Quite dumb?
Dead? Dead? A tomb
Must cover thy sweet eyes.
These lily lips,
This cherry nose,
These yellow cowslip cheeks

Are gone, are gone.
Lovers, make moan!
His eyes were green as leeks.
O °Sisters Three,
Come, come to me,
With hands as pale as milk.
Lay them in gore,
Since you have shore
With shears his thread of silk.
Tongue, not a word:
Come, trusty sword,
Come, blade, my breast imbrue!

She stabs herself.

And farewell, friends:
Thus Thisbe ends.
Adieu, adieu, adieu.

She dies.

Epilogue. Dance.

FINIS

4

Theatres and Scenery

Scenery is fine — but human nature is finer.

John Keats (1818)

It might be a fight like you see on the screen,
A swain getting slain for the love of a queen,
Some great Shakespearean scene
Where a ghost and a prince meet
And everyone ends in mincemeat.

Howard Dietz (1952)

'Sit in a full theatre,' marvelled the playwright John Webster in 1615, 'and you will think you see so many lines drawn from the circumference of so many ears, whiles the actor is the centre.' The geometry of his appreciation shares its vocabulary with the skilful architects and builders responsible for the complicated polygonal structures of the Rose (1587) and Globe (1599), and the great square build of the Fortune (1600). But the visual basis of his image – so strongly reminiscent of the diagrams recently published in the Museum of London's official archaeological report of Bankside excavations – risks overlooking the detail that it is to 'so many *ears*' that Webster's central actor projects his range. For all the lavish costumes of the tiring-house, English theatregoers have been *audiences* ever since this period (an era that habitually spoke of going to *hear* rather than *see* a play), while their French cousins obdurately remain *spectateurs*, true to the Ancient Greek etymology of the word 'theatre' (θέᾱτρον: 'a place for viewing').

109

So when Bottom awakes from his own midsummer night's dream, claiming that the 'eye of man hath not heard, the ear of man hath not seen' its like before, there is perhaps more to the comedy of its ridiculous confusion than meets the eye – or ear.

Even at the brand-new Globe, the Chorus of *Henry V* repeatedly enlists the 'imaginary forces' of its audience to supplement its sumptuous costumes, dramatic stage-effects, and huge cast-list. Indeed, it has been noticed that the constant disparagement of 'this wooden O' and its 'vile and raggèd foils' deliberately enhances the formidable odds against which Henry's Agincourt campaign is fought, recruiting its attentive audience's imagination to help win his Famous Victories, and ultimately enlisting their patriotic applause as active participants in the illusion of its triumph. As we have mentioned, *Henry V* is one of three candidates for the role of the Globe's inaugurating production in 1599, each of which differently exploits the wooden O's design.

Julius Caesar, known to have been performed 'in the house with the thatched roof' that September, shared with *Henry V* both its large cast of roles (numbering around fifty) and a still larger cast of thousands in the yard and galleries around its stage – whose crowded, attentive presence must have lent immeasurable force to the great public scenes of its tragedy. At the same time, visitors to London's playhouses were frequently struck by their architectural resemblance to 'Roman work', built 'in the Ancient Roman way', an impression reinforced by the pillars or columns (painted to imitate marble) that supported the canopy over part of the stage. The story of Julius Caesar – then widely believed to have built the nearby Tower of London – must therefore have seemed an appropriate vehicle with which to launch the Globe, the newest and so far most splendid example of such architecture.

Unless, that is, it was *As You Like It* that was chosen to open proceedings there, deliberately foregrounding the new theatre's intimate acoustics in the songs, dances, and music it features. Parallels have indeed been drawn between the sounding chamber of the 'wooden O' and the stringed instruments played within it – like the 'many lines drawn from the circumference of so many ears' Webster described. That play's most famous speech ('All the world's a stage...') certainly amplified the symbolic force of the Globe's name, and the medieval world-view that, for all its neo-classical pillars, underlay its architectural symbolism. With all human life paraded on the stage, it was an obvious instinct to locate Hell, via a trap-door, in the Underworld beneath (the 'cellarage' where the Ghost of Old Hamlet was shortly to stalk), and Heaven somewhere overhead. Literally overhead, in fact, since it was a wooden canopy, known as 'the heavens', gorgeously painted on its underside with the constellations of the zodiac, that those fake-marble pillars supported.

The custom-built playhouses of the 1570s to '90s inherited a theological framework from the old Morality plays, of the sort staged as the play-within-the-play in *Sir Thomas More*, by which Mankind, Everyman, or Youth sought salvation against the temptations of the Devil – the villainous 'Vice' that seduced him to damnation, and whose profile is clearly discernible in Richard III ('Thus, like the formal Vice, Iniquity, / I moralize two meanings in one word', 3.1), Iago, and even 'that villainous, abominable misleader of Youth' in *Henry IV, Part One*: 'Falstaff, that old white-bearded Satan' (2.4). 'What should such fellows as I do,' asks Hamlet, 'crawling between earth and heaven?' (3.1). The same cosmic architecture profoundly informs the fate of both Richard II (whose tragedy is the closest thing to a Christian Passion Shakespeare ever wrote) and Marlowe's Doctor Faustus (for whose play Henslowe's inventory included a 'hell-mouth'). It is in part for this reason that our expectations of a 'set' are largely anachronistic to Elizabethan playgoing: the gorgeous decoration of the theatre itself, the stunning costumes of its actors, and the sheer force of the English language all pre-empted the need for any 'realistic' scenery. Those pillars at the Globe, for example, served by turns to furnish the palatial interiors of *Henry V*, lend a suitably Roman backdrop to *Julius Caesar*, and supply a couple of convenient tree-trunks in the Forest of Arden for Orlando's pinned-up verses in *As You Like It*. To some, however, the Globe's very location among Southwark's other 'houses of resort in the suburbs' – its pubs, brothels, gamblers' dens and baiting-pits – was enough to equate it with vice (in its modern sense), and a queasy awareness of that proximity regularly surfaces in Shakespeare's work, in plays that oscillate between pubs and palaces, brothels and battlefields, country and court.

It used to be said, in the days before CGI, Blu-Ray, and 3D-HD-TV, that the pictures are always better on radio – to the 'mind's eye' that Hamlet mentions. Shakespeare's words, in plays first performed in natural light, subject to the vagaries of the English weather, and through-run on a largely bare stage, continue to prove that old-fashioned maxim true.

Theatreland

Then as now, London's playhouses were a magnet for foreign tourists – which is why so many of the detailed eye-witness accounts of the Elizabethan stage took some time to surface from various European archives. The Dutch tourist Johannes (or Jan) de Witt visited London in around 1596, and showed the detailed notes of his trip to his old friend Arend van Buchell on his return home. Van Buchell copied some of these into his own commonplace book – where he also redrew de Witt's sketch of the Swan theatre – and it was this manuscript that was discovered in the library of the University of Utrecht in 1888. De Witt's original – dating from before the demolition of the Theater and its reconstruction as the Globe in 1599 – has never been found. At best an amateur copy of an amateur sketch, the 'de Witt' drawing is nevertheless the closest thing we have to an image of a theatre's interior from Shakespeare's lifetime. A distorted snapshot it may be, but what is immediately clear is that what caught the visitor's eye on stage were the two rear doors to the tiring-house, flanked in his eyeline by the twin pillars; the rudimentary set (here simply a bench); and the detailed costumes, hats, props (and beard) of the three actors shown – with no scenery at all to suggest what sort of scene they were playing.

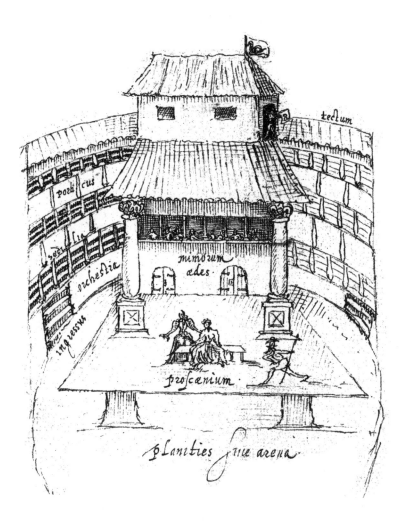

from Johannes de Witt's 'Observations of London' (c. 1596), from the Latin:

There are four amphitheatres in London of notable beauty, which from their diverse signs bear diverse names. In each of them a different play is daily exhibited to the populace. The two more magnificent of these are situated southward of the Thames, and from the signs suspended before them are called the Rose and the Swan. The two others [the Theater and the Curtain] are outside the City towards the north on the main road which issues through the Episcopal Gate commonly known as Bishopsgate [...] Of all the theatres, however, the largest and most magnificent is that one of which the sign is the swan, called in the vernacular the Swan Theatre, for it accommodates in its seats three thousand people, and is built of a mass of flint stones (of which there is a prodigious supply in Britain), and supported by wooden columns painted in such excellent imitation of marble that is able to deceive even the most enquiring eye. Since its form resembles that of a Roman work, I have made a sketch of it above.

'Heavens' above

The wooden canopy thrust midway across the stage, and supported by those mock Roman pillars, was known as the 'heavens', and seems to have been a common feature of Elizabethan theatre design – at least since the revamp of the Rose in 1592. De Witt's drawing of the Swan (built around 1595) shows it at eye-level or above (which suggests he had a seat in the equivalent of 'the gods'), and the surviving builders' contract for the Fortune – commissioned in January 1600 following the triumphant construction of the Globe the previous summer, and from the same architect – specifies the inclusion of a 'shadow or cover over the said stage... contrived and fashioned like unto the stage of the said playhouse called the Globe'. Shakespeare shared with his fellow actors a unique perspective on that zodiac ceiling (a bard's-eye view?), which repeatedly surfaces in his characters' stray allusions to the 'covering sky' (Leontes), 'painted with unnumber'd sparks' (Julius Caesar) – and surely also colours the reflection, in Sonnet 15, that 'this huge stage presenteth nought but shows / Whereon the stars in secret influence comment'. Hamlet's disgust at the world cannot but fixate upon the superficial glories of the Globe.

Hamlet (1600–1), 2.2:

HAMLET. I have of late — but wherefore I know not — lost all my mirth, forgone all custom of exercises; and indeed it goes so heavily with my disposition that this goodly frame the earth seems to me a sterile °promontory, this most excellent canopy the air, look you, this brave o'erhanging firmament, this majestical roof fretted with golden fire, why, it appears no other thing to me than a foul and pestilent congregation of vapours. What a piece of work is a man! How noble in reason, how infinite in faculty! In form and moving how express and admirable, in action how like an angel, in apprehension how like a god! The beauty of the world, the paragon of animals! And yet, to me, what is this quintessence of dust? Man delights not me.

Dust to dust... and, in time, ashes to ashes. The 1599 Globe was built with a thatched roof that sparked its destruction in June 1613. 'See the world's ruins! Nothing but the piles / Left!' joked Ben Jonson grimly, when fire destroyed his own library: 'And wit since to cover it with tiles' (see below, p. 141). By that time, however, Shakespeare and his company were established performers, since 1609, in the newly acquired private theatre across the river at Blackfriars, where audiences were smaller, but ticket prices higher. Performances continued at both venues, but the availability of an indoor theatre extended the commercial season into the winter months. It is difficult to imagine that Ariel's description of an old man's tears of joy in *The Tempest*, played at both, is not somehow related to the chilly spectacle, familiar to modern visitors to the reconstructed Globe, of rain dripping from the roof of a by then somewhat elderly theatre.

The Tempest (1612), 5.1:

ARIEL.   The King,
   His brother, and yours, abide all three distracted,
   And the remainder mourning over them,
   Brimful of sorrow and dismay; but chiefly
   Him that you term'd, sir, 'the good old lord Gonzalo':
   His tears run down his beard like winter's drops
   From eaves of reeds.

'The roar of the greasepaint, the smell of the crowd'

It was a 1960s musical that reversed the usual theatrical cliché ('the smell of the greasepaint, the roar of the crowd') – a piece of Broadway cynicism even more appropriate to the days before modern sanitation. The 'foul and pestilent congregation of vapours' at which Hamlet turns up his nose was a common theme in the earlier competition between the public and private theatres, then a straightforward rivalry between adult companies like Shakespeare's at the Globe, and those of the boy-actors (Hamlet's 'eyrie of children'), at the Blackfriars or St Paul's (to which Marston's theatregoer refers below). Otherwise closely faithful to his source, Thomas North's translation of Plutarch, Shakespeare invented the vivid (and site-specific?) detail of Casca's disgust at the 'stinking breath' of the ignorant crowd.

Julius Caesar (1599), 1.2:

CASCA. And then he offered it the third time; he put it the
   third time by; and still as he refused it, the rabblement
   hooted, and clapped their °chopped hands, and threw
   up their sweaty night-caps, and uttered such a deal of
   stinking breath because Caesar refused the crown that
   it had almost choked Caesar, for he swooned and fell
   down at it. And for mine own part, I durst not laugh,
   for fear of opening my lips and receiving the bad air.

CASSIUS. But soft, I pray you. What, did Caesar swoon?

CASCA. He fell down in the marketplace, and foamed at mouth, and was speechless.

BRUTUS. 'Tis very like. He hath the °falling sickness.

CASSIUS. No, Caesar hath it not; but you, and I,
And honest Casca, we have the falling sickness.

CASCA. I know not what you mean by that; but, I am sure Caesar fell down. If the °tag-rag people did not clap him and hiss him, according as he pleased and displeased them, as they use to do the players in the theatre, I am no true man.

John Marston, *Jack Drum's Entertainment* (1600), Act 5:

SIR EDWARD. I saw the Children of St Paul's last night,
And troth, they pleas'd me pretty, pretty well:
The apes in time will do it handsomely.

PLANET. I'faith, I like the audience that frequenteth there
With much applause: a man shall not be chok'd
With the stench of garlic, nor be pasted
To the °barmy jacket of a beer-brewer.

The second-oldest profession

Shakespeare remained acutely aware that the services he offered shared a clientele in the suburban neighbourhood of the theatres with those wishing to satisfy more urgent appetites and desires. The accusation of 'prostituting one's talent', or even of being a 'media whore', still sting. Shakespeare was alive to that shame, as witness the two Sonnets that – or so it is generally agreed – most directly reflect upon their author's career as an actor and author: as an actor for the 'motley' coat of the various parts he has paraded 'here and there' in London's public theatres (those 'public means' that have sponsored coarse behaviour); and as an author for the sale to the highest bidder of his most heartfelt verse ('sold cheap what is most dear'), his fingers as inky as 'the dyer's hand' with the stain of his socially inferior trade.

from Sonnets 110 and 111 (published 1609):

> Alas, 'tis true, I have gone here and there,
> And made myself a °motley to the view,
> °Gor'd mine own thoughts, sold cheap what is most dear,
> Made old offences of affections new.
> Most true it is that I have look'd on truth
> °Askance and strangely.
>
> O, for my sake °do you with Fortune chide,
> The guilty goddess of my harmful deeds,
> That did not better for my life provide
> Than public means, which public manners breeds;
> Thence comes it that my name receives a °brand,
> And almost thence my nature is subdued
> To what it works in, like the dyer's hand.

Red light and green room

Hamlet echoes his creator in savagely bemoaning how he 'Must like a whore unpack my heart with words / And fall a-cursing like a very drab [= *whore*]' (2.2), and such associations of street-walker to board-treader were more than a commonplace since both plied their trade in a common place: the insalubrious suburbs beyond the boundaries or jurisdiction of the City of London authorities. 'Dwell I but in the suburbs / Of your good pleasure?' asks Portia of her neglectful husband in *Julius Caesar*: 'If it be no more, / Portia is Brutus' harlot, not his wife' (2.1). Sir John Davies's thumbnail sketch of Fuscus, a swarthy (or so his name translates) and typically louche play-goer, spells out that association.

Sir John Davies, Epigram 39 (1594):

> Fuscus is free, and hath the world at will,
> Yet in the course of life that he doth lead
> He's like a horse which turning round a mill
> Doth always in the self-same circle tread:
> First he doth rise at ten, and at eleven
> He goes to Jill's, where he doth eat till one,
> Then sees a play till six, and sups at seven,
> And after supper straight to bed is gone,
> And there till ten next day he doth remain,
> And then he dines, then sees a comedy,
> And then he sups, and goes to bed again.
> Thus round he runs without variety:
>> Save that sometimes he comes not to the play
>> But falls into a whorehouse by the way.

Marston's joke (above, p. 92) about a dreadful playwright's 'name at a play-door' being as dangerous as 'a printed bill on a plague-door' – and so spelling box-office poison – was a black one indeed. Although the science wasn't yet fully understood, it was nevertheless recognized that in times of plague, large congregations of people increased the chance of contagion, and theatres were periodically closed for this reason throughout Shakespeare's career. The circumstance forced acting companies on provincial tour (Edward Alleyn writing to his wife from Bristol in July 1593, 'hoping in God, though the sickness be round about you, yet by his mercy it may escape your house'), and playwrights to expand their poetic horizons: Shakespeare's narrative poem *Venus and Adonis* was entered for publication in the Stationers' Register that April. Such measures played into the hands of those contemporary moral guardians who equated *play* with *plague*,* locating the source of the disease in God's displeasure at such dens of iniquity. A government directive of 1596 sought to suppress 'houses of unlawful and disorderly resort'; and following yet another outbreak of plague in 1603, a

---

* See, definitively, Christopher Ricks, '*Doctor Faustus* and Hell on Earth', in his *Essays in Appreciation* (Clarendon Press, 1996), pp. 1–18.

proclamation was issued by the new King requiring the immediate demolition of suburban houses frequented by 'dissolute and dangerous persons'. These measures 'for the supplanting and depopulating of vice' have been linked to Shakespeare's more measured account of Puritan zeal and human folly in the play he wrote that year.

Measure for Measure (1603–4), 1.2:

POMPEY. You have not heard of the proclamation, have you?

MRS OVERDONE. What proclamation, man?

POMPEY. All houses in the suburbs of Vienna must be plucked down.

MRS OVERDONE. And what shall become of those in the city?

POMPEY. They shall °stand for seed; they had gone down too, but that a wise burgher put in for them.

MRS OVERDONE. But shall all our houses of resort in the suburbs be pulled down?

POMPEY. To the ground, mistress.

MRS OVERDONE. Why, here's a change indeed in the commonwealth! What shall become of me?

POMPEY. Come, fear not you: good counsellors lack no clients. Though you °change your place, you need not change your trade.

A bloody damnation…

The Tragical History of Doctor Faustus – the story of the scholar for whom the world is not enough – enjoyed repeated revivals for the long duration of Shakespeare's career, finally inspiring his own magician Prospero's curtain-call ('I'll drown my book'). The stagecraft of Marlowe's final scene orders '*Music*

while the Throne descends' for the Good Angel, and specifies that
'*Hell is discovered*' by the Bad Angel before Faustus speaks his
last. But despite the expensive carpentry Henslowe commissioned for the 'throne', the painted 'hell-mouth' later listed
among his props, the 'roll'd bullet' and firecrackers used to
denote thunder and lightning, the striking of a backstage bell,
and the carcass of meat later used to display his disjointed
limbs – despite all this, it is Marlowe's words that transform
the otherwise bare boards of this early wooden O into the
clock-face of its hero's final hour of life.

Christopher Marlowe, *Doctor Faustus* (c. 1590–92), 5.2:

FAUSTUS. Ah, Faustus,
   Now hast thou but one bare hour to live,
   And then thou must be damn'd perpetually.
   Stand still, you ever-moving spheres of Heaven,
   That time may cease, and midnight never come;
   Fair Nature's eye, rise, rise again and make
   Perpetual day; or let this hour be but
   A year, a month, a week, a natural day,
   That Faustus may repent and save his soul!
   °*O lente lente currite noctis equi.*
   The stars move still, time runs, the clock will strike,
   The Devil will come, and Faustus must be damn'd.
   O, I'll leap up to my God! Who pulls me down?
   See, see where Christ's blood streams in the
      firmament!
   One drop would save my soul — half a drop. Ah, my
      Christ! [...]
   Curst be the parents that engender'd me!
   No, Faustus: curse thyself — curse Lucifer
   That hath depriv'd thee of the joys of Heaven.

                         The clock striketh twelve.

   O, it strikes, it strikes! Now, body, turn to air,
   Or Lucifer will bear thee quick to Hell!

                         Thunder and lightning.

O soul, be chang'd into little water-drops,
And fall into the ocean, ne'er be found.
My God, my God! Look not so fierce on me!

Enter DEVILS.

Adders and serpents, let me breathe awhile!
Ugly Hell, gape not! Come not, Lucifer!
I'll burn my books! — Ah, Mephistophilis!

Exeunt DEVILS *with* FAUSTUS.

... and a creaking apotheosis

It was a platitude of Classical literature – of the sort Shakespeare greedily devoured in Ovid's *Metamorphoses*, for example – that heroes be borne aloft into the sky at their death, there to be transformed from mortal into god, or else transfigured into an astronomical constellation (like the ones painted on the underside of the 'heavens'). Cleopatra's instructions to hoist Antony's dying body from the main stage to the gallery where she awaits him, towards the end of their play, seems a deliberate ridicule of those conventions – no wafting or gliding here! But the clink, and sweat, and effort of the Globe's rope-and-pulley system, together with a characteristically simple language, results in even greater poignancy.

Antony and Cleopatra (1607), 4.15:

CLEOPATRA.   But come, come, Antony —
    Help me, my women — we must draw thee up.
    Assist, good friends!

ANTONY.   O, quick, or I am gone!

CLEOPATRA. Here's sport indeed! How heavy weighs my lord!
    Our strength is all gone into °heaviness:
    That makes the weight. Had I great °Juno's power,
    The strong-wing'd Mercury should fetch thee up

And set thee by Jove's side. Yet come a little;
Wishers were ever fools. O, come, come, come.

They heave ANTONY *aloft to* CLEOPATRA.

And welcome, welcome! Die when thou hast liv'd;
°Quicken with kissing. Had my lips that power,
Thus would I wear them out.

ALL THE GUARD. Ah, heavy sight!

ANTONY. I am dying, Egypt, dying.

The mind's eye

'My father,' muses Hamlet to his old friend, 'methinks I see
my father' – which comes as something a shock to Horatio,
who has just seen – along with thousands of witnesses in the
Globe – the apparition of the old King's ghost. 'Where, my
lord?' he asks (strengthened to 'Oh, where, my lord?' in the
Folio). 'In my mind's eye, Horatio,' comes the reply. In the
play Shakespeare drafted – preserved in its Second Quarto
edition, but cut from the performed script that the Folio supplies – the moment of Horatio's confusion is lent an extra
shiver by the fact that Hamlet uncannily uses the very same
expression that Horatio himself had earlier used, shortly
before the ghost's second appearance ('A mote it is to trouble
the mind's eye'). Shakespeare had earlier meditated on the pri-
mal force of the imagination, in a famous sequence (below),
which he evidently added as an afterthought in his working
papers, cramming the words into the margin to the eventual
confusion of the printer of the play's First Quarto (1600),
where the passage is mislined.

A Midsummer Night's Dream (1595), 5.1:

THESEUS. The poet's eye, in a fine frenzy rolling,
   Doth glance from heaven to earth, from earth to heaven;
   And as imagination bodies forth

The forms of things unknown, the poet's pen
Turns them to shapes and gives to airy nothing
A local habitation and a name.

As we have already seen, the dramatist and poet Thomas Heywood was one of Shakespeare's earliest – and humblest – fans. (He once publicly complained that two of his own poems had been wrongly ascribed to Shakespeare in a sloppily produced anthology, 'but I must acknowledge my lines not worth his patronage'.) The Chorus he wrote to his own brilliant domestic tragedy – in the rhyme-scheme of Shakespeare's Sonnets, no less – spells out the details of the superficial 'twig', 'barren' setting, and 'thin water' of the bare stage that must stand for the trees, fields, and wine of the full illusion he is about to present. The difference between the Choruses of Heywood and of Shakespeare ('But pardon, gentles all…') is that Heywood seems almost to have meant it.

Thomas Heywood, The Prologue to *A Woman Killed with Kindness* (1603):

CHORUS. I come but like a harbinger, being sent
    To tell you what these preparations mean.
    Look for no glorious state: our muse is bent
    Upon a barren subject, a bare scene.
    We could °afford this twig a timber tree,
    Whose strength might boldly on your favours build;
    Our °russet, tissue; drone, a honey-bee;
    Our barren plot, a large and spacious field;
    Our coarse fare, banquets; our thin water, wine;
    Our brook, a sea; our bat's eyes, eagle's sight;
    Our poet's dull and earthy muse, divine;
    Our ravens, doves; our crow's black feathers, white.
      But gentle thoughts, when they may °give the foil,
      Save them that yield, and spare where they may
        spoil.

The power of the imagination

Despite the full resources of the Globe playhouse in its pomp
– the brilliant costumes, the finesse of its music, the tour-de-
force acting from 'the best actors in the world' and their
fluently choreographed hired men, the range of its stage-effects
and naturalistic props, the intoxicating transport of its audiences' imaginations all over the known world, in time and in
space, from Venice and Verona to Elsinore and Ancient Rome
– despite all such assets, Shakespeare's most determined vision
of his theatrical craft reduces to a single scene. Gloucester is
blind. The man he does not know to be his son Edgar is
dressed in the humblest of clothes. The sea really *is* far away.
The surface of the stage he believes himself climbing really *is*
level. Modern drama is born.

King Lear (1605), 4.6:

GLOUCESTER. When shall I come to th' top of that same hill?

EDGAR. You do climb up it now. Look how we labour.

GLOUCESTER. Methinks the ground is even.

EDGAR.   Horrible steep.
    Hark, do you hear the sea?

GLOUCESTER.   No, truly.

EDGAR. Why then, your other senses grow imperfect
    By your eyes' anguish.

GLOUCESTER.   So may it indeed.
    Methinks thy voice is alter'd and thou speak'st
    In better phrase and matter than thou didst.

EDGAR. You're much deceived: in nothing am I chang'd
    But in my garments.

GLOUCESTER.   Methinks you're better spoken.

EDGAR. Come on, sir, here's the place. Stand still: how
        fearful
    And dizzy 'tis to cast one's eyes so low!
    The crows and choughs that wing the midway air

Show scarce so gross as beetles. Halfway down
Hangs one that gathers °samphire, dreadful trade;
Methinks he seems no bigger than his head.
The fishermen that walk upon the beach
Appear like mice, and yond tall anchoring barque
Diminished to her °cock, her cock a buoy
Almost too small for sight. The murmuring surge
That on th'°unnumber'd idle pebble chafes
Cannot be heard so high. I'll look no more,
Lest my brain turn and the °deficient sight
Topple down headlong.

GLOUCESTER.   Set me where you stand.

EDGAR. Give me your hand: you are now within a foot
    Of th'extreme verge. For all beneath the moon
    Would I not leap upright.

GLOUCESTER.   Let go my hand. […]

                                        GLOUCESTER *falls.*

EDGAR. What are you, sir?

GLOUCESTER.   Away, and let me die.

EDGAR. Hadst thou been aught but gossamer, feathers, air,
    So many fathom down precipitating,
    Thou'dst °shiver'd like an egg; but thou dost breathe,
    Hast heavy substance, bleed'st not, speak'st, art sound.
    Ten masts °at each make not the altitude
    Which thou hast perpendicularly fell.
    Thy life's a miracle. Speak yet again.

GLOUCESTER. But have I fallen, or no?

EDGAR. From the dread summit of this chalky °bourn.
    Look up a-height: the shrill-gorg'd lark so far
    Cannot be seen or heard. Do but look up.

GLOUCESTER. Alack, I have no eyes.

5

Fluffs, Prompts, Cues, and Snags

The awful consciousness that one is the sole object of attention to that immense space, lined as it were with human intellect from top to bottom, and on all sides round, may perhaps be imagined but can never be described, and by me can never be forgotten.

Sarah Siddons (1782)

WABASH. °'W-w-w-w-was th-th-this th-th-the f-f-f-ace—'

HENSLOWE (*unexpectedly*). Very good, Mr Wabash. Excellent. Report to the property master. — My tailor. Wants to be an actor. I have a few debts here and there. Well, that seems to be everybody.

Shakespeare in Love (1999)

It is any actor's worst nightmare – worse even than forgetting his lines. Striding alone onstage, clad in black and with a prop-book in hand, he turns to the audience, addresses himself to speak, allows a short pause, and then – '*To be, or not to be…*' comes the loudly whispered and very much unwanted cue from the over-eager offstage prompter. As if the butterfly nerves and constant insecurity weren't enough to contend with. The comedy of Jack Benny's face during this torture – brilliantly cast as a cuckolded actor in Lubitsch's *To Be Or Not To Be* (1942) – lies beyond words to describe.* Still harder to describe (because

---

* Michael Billington's description of his 'baffled feminine outrage' comes close. See *One Night Stands* (Nick Hern Books, 2001), p. 31.

preserved only in words) are those frequent occasions when Shakespeare made similar play with the hitches, snags, and fluffs that have always accompanied the business of 'live' theatre.

His script has been delivered to the company; it has been cast, rehearsed, revised, and officially approved; cue-parts have been copied from its certified 'theatre-book', and these have been distributed among the actors to be learned; some new costumes have been bought, and some old ones adapted and fitted; props have been selected or procured – and the diagram of its action, detailing the necessary entrances and props, has been noted on the poster-sized 'platt' now pegged up back-stage. It's nearly two o'clock, the trumpeter is blowing his second fanfare from the upper gallery, the audience is settling, some last-minute cuts have been explained, and now the third blast is being sounded, and… you're on!

The language – and experience – of his theatre-of-the-world repeatedly struck Shakespeare as true to the lives we all lead, lives that – like the performances of 'all the men and women' he imagined there – often tend to go a bit wrong. (Granted, a bit more wrong for some than for others, as Titus Andronicus might have pointed out to Viola.) When we encounter a crisis in real life, it is strange how often we feel the moment to be some-how fictional, theatrical, 'unreal'. The Bastard in *King John*, for example, likens the defiant citizens assembled on the battle-ments of their besieged town to the spectators 'in a theatre, whence they gape and point / At your industrious scenes and acts of death' (2.1) – an early example of Brecht's 'Alienation-effect', according to some (by which an audience's sudden self-consciousness objectifies the action they are seeing onstage). Well, maybe so. Or else, perhaps, such moments – as when Warwick ('the King-maker') rebukes his troops for their inertia on the field of battle, 'as if the tragedy / Were play'd in jest by counterfeiting actors' (*Henry VI, Part Three* (1592), 2.3) – in fact catch in their very re-enactment the strange italics of momentous events. Shakespeare profoundly appreciated this theatrical sense of experience, often building into his scripts a knife-edge awareness that things were happening beyond their jurisdiction; as they so often do, of course, in the clutch of am-dram disasters his Comedies so enjoyably contrive, which remain among the best in a crowded field. Bad actors have always been a fairly easy target for good actors to satirize, of course. What is remarkable is how often Shakespeare returned to the theme in his Tragedies, in those moments when the human suffering they depict gains extra dimension by the sudden backstage glimpse of a performance going wrong, in the theatre of life in which we all play our parts.

Of all the hundreds of roles in his dozens of plays, however, it is probably the jealous husband Ford in *The Merry Wives of Windsor* (3.2) – a part conceivably played by Shakespeare himself in what by all accounts was a more than usually rushed and hectic production – who best reflects the turbulent rush that has been dreaded and relished by all theatre companies ever since: 'The clock gives me my cue!'

First-night nerves

The sheer toil of learning so many lines for the constant grind of performing a new or half-remembered play every day must surely have resulted in a higher incidence of 'drying' – or being 'out' – in Shakespeare's theatre than in today's. Such glitches, then as now, were smoothed over by prompts from the wings by the 'book-keeper' (or 'stage-keeper'), who followed the complicatedly annotated and approved text of a play's script in its so-called 'theatre-copy' (or 'prompt-book'). The last-minute inserts, panics, and freezes of such performances are nicely parodied at the outset of the third and final play of a trilogy written and performed at St John's College, Cambridge, in the successive winter seasons of 1599–1602.

Anon., *The Second Part of the Return from Parnassus* (1601–2), Prologue:

> *Enter* BOY *as Prologue.*
>
> BOY. 'Spectators — we will — act a — Comedy...'
>
> > *Long silence.*

Enter the STAGE-KEEPER, *with the prompt-book.*

STAGE-KEEPER. A pox on't, this book hath it not in't! You would be whipped, you rascal! You must be sitting up all night at cards when you should be conning your part!

BOY. It's °all long of you I could not get my part a night or two before, that I might sleep on't.

The STAGE-KEEPER *carries the* BOY *away under his arm.*

The absurdity may have been borrowed from the enjoyable fiasco the boy Moth makes of the opening section of the Lords' pageant in *Love's Labour's Lost*, despite the frantic prompts from one of its authors, now seated out front. Moth's stage-directed entrance *'with a speech'* suggests that he brandishes the scroll of his prologue in his hand – though what follows demonstrates that the lines he has learned from it are easily thrown by an audience's heckles.

Love's Labour's Lost (1595), 5.2:

BOYET. The trumpet sounds. Be mask'd: the masquers come.

The PRINCESS *and her* LADIES *put on masks. Music.*

Enter MOTH *with a speech, and the* KING *and his* LORDS *in masks and costumes.*

MOTH. 'All hail, the richest beauties on the earth —'

BOYET. Beauties no richer than rich °taffeta.

MOTH. 'A holy °parcel of the fairest dames

The LADIES *turn their backs to him.*

That ever turn'd their — backs to mortal views —'

BEROWNE. 'Their *eyes*', villain! 'Their *eyes*'!

MOTH. 'That ever turn'd their *eyes* to mortal views:

Out —'

BOYET. True! Out indeed!

MOTH. 'Out of your favours, heavenly spirits, vouchsafe Not to behold —'

BEROWNE. '*Once* to behold', rogue!

MOTH. '*Once* to behold with your sun-beamèd eyes…
    with your sun-beamèd eyes —'

BOYET. They will not answer to that epithet:
    You were best call it '*daughter*-beamèd eyes'!

MOTH. They do not °mark me, and that brings me out.

BEROWNE. Is this your perfectness? Be gone, you rogue!

                                 Exit MOTH.

Stagefright

Moth's muffed Prologue, along with the butterflies associated with all theatrical performance, remained close to Shakespeare's heart throughout his career, whether from close observation of his fellow actors or from personal experience. Duke Theseus's generous description of the 'premeditated welcomes' botched through stagefright suggests an immediate familiarity with the civic pageants, formal welcomes, and private performances that were the stock-in-trade of an Elizabethan actor, whether amateur or professional. According to some scholars, *A Midsummer Night's Dream* may itself have been written for the occasion of a private aristocratic wedding, which would lend an extra layer of flattery to Theseus's magnanimity – and a further comic dimension to the pig's ear Peter Quince subsequently makes of the 'practis'd accents' of his own Prologue to *Pyramus and Thisbe* (see above, p. 10).

A Midsummer Night's Dream (1595), 5.1:

THESEUS. Where I have come, great °clerks have purposèd
    To greet me with premeditated welcomes;
    Where I have seen them shiver and look pale,
    Make periods in the midst of sentences,
    Throttle their practis'd accent in their fears,
    And in conclusion, dumbly have broke off,

Not paying me a welcome. Trust me, sweet,
Out of this silence yet I pick'd a welcome,
And in the modesty of fearful duty
I read as much as from the rattling tongue
Of saucy and audacious eloquence.
Love, therefore, and tongue-tied simplicity
In least speak most to my capacity.

EGEUS. So please your grace, the Prologue is address'd.

THESEUS. Let him approach.

If Shakespeare had closely observed cases of stagefright in others, his Sonnet 23 seems to speak from somewhere inside himself. Unable – as if! – to express in words the love he feels for his friend, the speaker compares his tongue-tied plight to the likes of Moth and Quince (an 'unperfect actor' can mean either a *mediocre* one, or one that isn't yet *word-perfect* in his lines), thrown off-script by the strength of his feelings, and the responsibility it entails. Reduced to silence, he refers the addressee to the full of eloquence of 'my books' – whether the collection of Sonnets we are now reading or the 'prompt-books' of his plays, to which such occasions of 'drying' were always referred; and then to the 'dumb presagers' that preface a play's action in the form of the so-called Dumb Show (see above, p. 14), where the spectators of an audience can truly 'hear with eyes'.

Sonnet 23 (published 1609):

As an unperfect actor on the stage
Who with his fear is put besides his part,
Or some fierce thing replete with too much rage,
Whose °strength's abundance weakens his own heart:
So I, for fear of trust, forget to say
The perfect ceremony of love's rite,
And in mine own love's strength seem to decay,
O'ercharg'd with burden of mine own love's might.
O, let my books be then the eloquence
And dumb presagers of my speaking breast,

Who plead for love and look for recompense
More than that tongue that more hath more express'd.
O, learn to read what silent love hath writ!
To hear with eyes belongs to love's fine wit.

Quite when Shakespeare wrote this sonnet remains unknown. It is nonetheless intriguing that the perfect synopsis of its premise can be found in *Greene's Groatsworth of Wit* – the same posthumous miscellany that had accused him of being an 'upstart crow' (see above, p. 35).

from Greene's Groatsworth of Wit (1592):

> Lucanio, being so far in love as he persuaded himself without her grant he could not live, had a good °meaning to utter his mind, but wanting fit words he stood like a °truant that lacked a prompter, or a player that, being out of his part at his first entrance, is fain to have the book to speak what he should perform.

Drying

Perhaps aided by the semi-improvised nature of contemporary cue-part performance, Shakespeare's plays regularly offer the fleeting suspicion that an actor in its plot has wandered off-script, or otherwise requires prompting from the wings – much as one often finds oneself lost for words, struck dumb, or stunned into silence by real events. In *Julius Caesar*, for example, on the morning of the assassination, Portia abruptly packs off her servant to the Senate with a message for Brutus, but the boy obstinately refuses to leave. 'Why dost thou stay?' she asks crossly. 'To know my errand, madam,' comes the reply: in the anxiety of the moment she has forgotten to tell him what message it is he should convey (2.4). Similar, though in a different key, is Orlando's response to Rosalind's gift of a chain after his wrestling match in *As You Like It* (1.2) – or rather non-response, smitten and tongue-tied as he is ('a mere life-less block!') after falling in love with her at first sight. These are beautifully observed moments of human fluster – accentu-ated by the *frisson* in their earliest performances that the relevant actor has dried. And not simply then, as anyone who saw the 1989 National Theatre production of *Hamlet*, and Polonius's 'daringly stretched-out pause', still remembers. 'Great ad-lib, we thought,' wrote Harriet Walter: 'It was so star-tlingly natural that I had to look it up when I got home. It was all Shakespeare, and Michael Bryant played it to the hilt.'*

Hamlet (1600–1), 2.1:

POLONIUS. Mark you, your °party in converse (him you
    would sound)
  Having ever seen in the °prenominate crimes
  The youth you breathe of guilty, be assur'd
  He °closes with you in this consequence:
  'Good sir...', or so; or 'friend', or 'gentleman' —
  According to the phrase or the addition
  Of man and country —

REYNALDO.   Very good, my lord.

POLONIUS. And then, sir, does he this. He does... What
  was I about to say? By the mass, I was about to say
  something! Where did I leave?

REYNALDO. At 'closes in the consequence'.

POLONIUS. At 'closes in the consequence'? Ay, marry!
  He closes thus: 'I know the gentleman,
  I saw him yesterday' — or 'th'other day',
  Or then, or then, with such or such — 'and as you say,
  There *was* he gaming, there °o'ertook in's rouse,
  There falling out at tennis...'

The illusion of Polonius's drying ('all Shakespeare') is the more remarkable for appearing early on in one of his Tragedies

---

* Harriet Walter, *Other People's Shoes: Thoughts on Acting* (Nick Hern Books, 2003), p. 208. I saw that production twice myself, and Bryant somehow managed to catch me out both times.

– rather than as part of the amateur theatricals that so often conclude the Comedies. The sudden acknowledgement of the surrounding artifice of these stories – 'metatheatre', in the scholarly jargon – was one of Shakespeare's favourite devices. When Brabantio, for example, arrives with an armed platoon to arrest Othello for using witchcraft to seduce his daughter, the Moor forcefully reduces the emotional temperature by resisting such provocations, casting himself as an experienced actor, fully in charge of the scene he is playing: 'Hold your hands,' he instructs. 'Were it my cue to fight, I should have known it / Without a prompter' (1.2). That situation is perfectly reversed in the despairing words of a slightly later soldier-hero, the austere Coriolanus, whose vengeful resolution to conquer his native Rome begins to waver on hearing petitions for mercy from his wife. (His laconic self-possession is nicely caught here by the fact that his reference to forgetting his lines completes the formal metre of the line she begins.)

Coriolanus (1608), 5.3:

VIRGINIA. My lord and husband!

CORIOLANUS. These eyes are not the same I wore in Rome.

VIRGINIA. The sorrow that delivers us thus chang'd
    Makes you think so.

CORIOLANUS. Like a dull actor now
    I have forgot my part and I am out,
    Even to a full disgrace.

What's my motivation?

Revenge, like theatre, depends on successful imitation ('an eye for an eye, a tooth for a tooth'), so it is fitting that the stagestruck Prince Hamlet's self-rebuke for delaying his revenge arises from the feigned emotions of the Player's recital, whose 'cue for passion' (or signal for performance) is some mouldy old script about the Trojan War. Were such a brilliant actor to respond to a grievance as real as his own, he says here, no audience could bear the authenticity of his emoting. And so is born (see below, p. 154) the conceit of the play-within-the-play 'to catch the conscience of the King'.

Hamlet (1600–1), 2.2:

HAMLET. O, what a rogue and peasant slave am I!
  Is it not monstrous that this player here,
  But in a fiction, in a dream of passion,
  Could force his soul so to his own conceit
  That from her working all his °visage wann'd,
  Tears in his eyes, distraction in's aspèct,
  A broken voice, and his whole function suiting
  With forms to his conceit? And all for nothing!
  For °Hecuba!
  What's Hecuba to him, or he to Hecuba,
  That he should weep for her? What would he do,
  Had he the motive and the cue for passion
  That I have? He would drown the stage with tears
  And °cleave the general ear with horrid speech,
  Make mad the guilty and appal the °free,
  Confound the ignorant, and amaze indeed
  The very faculties of eyes and ears.

Another key component both of theatre and revenge is the faculty of memory, whether focused on the cue-scripts of an actor's intended performance or on the grievance of a revenger's. (This is perhaps why such great store is set in so many plays of the time on the concentrated incitement of a single prop: Hieronymo's 'bloody napkin', stained with his son's blood, in Kyd's *Spanish Tragedy*; Desdemona's handkerchief in Othello; the skull of Vindice's dead beloved in *The Revenger's Tragedy*.) 'Remember thee?' asks Hamlet of his father's shade, 'Ay, thou poor ghost, while memory holds a seat / In this distracted globe' (1.5). That pun (accentuated by the Folio edition's deftly capitalized 'Globe') is profound: Hamlet vows to remember his father for as long as memory plays a part in the workings of his mental turmoil – and for as long as there are tickets available for booking at the theatre box-office for the performance of his story. But memory was over-taxed in other ways – as the earliest-printed version of Hamlet's 'O what a rogue and peasant slave' demonstrates. Probably pieced together and paraphrased from faulty memory by the bit-part participants of an early performance, the following variant text carries a unique force of its own.

Hamlet (1600–1, First Quarto, 1603), 2.2:

HAMLET. Why, what a dunghill idiot slave am I!
 Why, these players here draw water from eyes:
 For Hecuba!
 Why, what is Hecuba to him, or he to Hecuba?
 What would he do °an if he had my loss?
 His father murder'd, and a crown bereft him?
 He would turn all his tears to drops of blood,
 Amaze the standers-by with his laments,
 Strike more than wonder in the judicial ears,
 Confound the ignorant, and make mute the wise.
 Indeed, his passion would be °general.

The show must go on

The messy manuscript bundle known as 'The Book of Sir Thomas More', which survives in the British Library, is misnamed, since the play was not performed until the twentieth century, and the 'prompt-book' it was intended to supply consequently never used on the Jacobethan stage. Written by five different authors (one of them Shakespeare), in two phases of composition between around 1593 and 1600, following strident intervention by the state censor, the play has recently received critical and popular applause, not least for the sophisticated portrayal of its hero, the wise and witty scholar forced to the scaffold by the integrity of his conscience. One of the play's best scenes is its own play-within-the-play: the aptly titled 'Interlude' of *The Marriage of Wit and Wisdom*, which More commissions from a troupe of players to entertain his eminent guests. But there is a hitch in the performance. The actor Luggins, who is playing the part of Good Counsel, has been delayed on his errand to pick up a 'long beard' from John Ogle (a famous Elizabethan haberdasher and wig-maker), and the production stalls. Until, that is, a surprise understudy emerges from the audience to improvise the role.

Anthony Munday et al., *Sir Thomas More* (1593–1600), 3.2:

LADY VANITY. 'For it hath been told me many a time
    That you would be seen in no such company as mine.'

WIT.   'Not Wit in the company of Lady Wisdom?
    O Jove, for what do I hither come?'

INCLINATION. 'Sir, she did this nothing else but to prove
    Whether a little thing would you move
    To be angry and fret.
    What °an if one said so,
    Let such trifling matters go,
    And with a kind kiss come out of her debt.'

                                                    Pause.

Enter another PLAYER.

    (*Aside.*) Is Luggins come yet with the beard?

PLAYER. No, faith, he is not come. Alas, what shall we do?

INCLINATION (*to the audience*). Forsooth, we can go no
    further till our fellow Luggins come, for he plays
    Good Counsel, and now he should enter to admonish
    Wit that this is Lady Vanity and not Lady Wisdom.

THOMAS MORE (*from the audience*). Nay, an it be no more
    but so, ye shall not °tarry at a stand for that. We'll not
    have a play marred for lack of a little good counsel!
    Till your fellow come, I'll give him the best counsel
    that I can. — Pardon me, my Lord Mayor, I love to be
    merry.

                            He climbs on to the stage.

'O Wit, thou art now °on the bow hand,
And °blindly in thine own opinion dost stand.
I tell thee, this naughty lewd Inclination
Does lead thee amiss in a very strange fashion.
This is not Wisdom, but Lady Vanity:
Therefore list to Good Counsel, and be rul'd by me.'

INCLINATION (*aside*). In troth, my lord, it is as right to
Luggins's part as can be! — Speak, Wit.

THOMAS MORE. Nay, we will not have our audience
disappointed if I can help it.

WIT.   'Art thou Good Counsel, and will tell me so?
Wouldst thou have Wit from Lady Wisdom go?
Thou art some deceiver, I tell thee verily,
In saying that this is Lady Vanity.'

THOMAS MORE. 'Wit, judge not things by the outward show:
The eye oft mistakes, right well you do know.
Good Counsel assures thee upon his honesty
That this is not Wisdom, but Lady Vanity.'

Enter LUGGINS *backstage with the beard.*

INCLINATION. O my lord, he is come! Now we shall go
forward.

THOMAS MORE (*to* LUGGINS). Art thou come? Well, fellow, I
have °holp to save thine honesty a little. Now, if thou
canst give Wit any better counsel than I have done,
spare not. There I leave him to thy mercy. —

But by this time, I am sure, our banquet's ready:
My lord and ladies, we will taste that first
And then they shall begin the play again,
Which, through the fellow's absence, and by me,
Instead of helping, hath been hinderèd.
Prepare against we come. Lights there, I say.
Thus fools oft times do help to mar the play.

Exeunt all but the PLAYERS.

Noises off

Some hitches are worse than others, of course, and Shakespeare's theatrical career in London was book-ended by two extraordinary accidents, one at the Rose, shortly before his arrival in the capital, and the second at the Globe, shortly before his permanent return to Stratford. The following extract from a letter dated November 1587 demonstrates that Alleyn's company, the Lord Admiral's Men, could on occasion *really* slay them in the aisles – or so the gossip went. The dating of Marlowe's plays is a notoriously thorny issue, but scholars have tentatively identified the cause of this fatal accident to the sequence given towards the end of the second of his vastly successful plays about the conquering tyrant Tamburlaine. (Since the play wasn't published until 1590, however, the stage-victim's place of execution may have been judiciously moved upstage.)

Christopher Marlowe, *Tamburlaine, Part Two* (1587–8), 5.1:

> *The* GOVERNOR OF BABYLON *appears hanging in chains on the city walls.*

AMYRAS. See now, my lord, how brave the captain hangs.

TAMBURLAINE. 'Tis brave indeed, my boy, well done.
Shoot first, my lord, and then the rest shall follow.

THERIDAMAS. Then have at him to begin withal.

> THERIDAMAS *shoots.*

GOVERNOR. Yet save my life and let this wound appease
The mortal fury of great Tamburlaine.

TAMBURLAINE. No, though °Asphaltis' lake were liquid gold,
And offer'd me as ransom for thy life,
Yet shouldst thou die — shoot at him all at once.

> *They shoot.*

from Philip Gawdy, letter to his father, November 1587:

> My Lord Admiral his men and players, having a device
> in their play to tie one of their fellows to a post and
> so to shoot him to death, having borrowed their

°calivers, one of the players' hands swerved; his
piece, being charged with a bullet, missed the fellow
he aimed at, and killed a child, and a woman great
with child forthwith, and hurt another man in the
head very sore. How they will answer it, I do not
study unless their profession were better, but in
Christianity I am very sorry for the chance; but God
His judgements are not to be searched nor enquired
of at man's hands. And yet I find by this an old
proverb verified: that [there] never comes more hurt
than comes of fooling.

'No longer since than yesterday,' reads another letter, written a
quarter-century later, on 30 June 1613, 'while Burbage his
company were acting at ye Globe the play of *Henry 8*, and there
shooting off certain chambers [= *gun-barrels*] in way of triumph, the fire catch'd & fasten'd upon the thatch of the ye
house and there burned so furiously as it consumed the whole
house & all in less than two hours...' The most disastrous
sound-effect in theatrical history was cued in the early banquet
scene of Shakespeare and Fletcher's *Henry VIII*, barely half an
hour into the performance. 'But O, those reeds!' wrote Ben
Jonson of that perilously vulnerable thatched roof, which – so
he claims – he witnessed 'with [= *by*] two poor chambers
taken in / And raz'd'. The play's original title was the altogether
more enigmatic *All Is True* – as the sardonic chorus of the
anonymous ballad written about the disaster pressed home. No
wonder that Heminge and Condell (the ballad's rather dodgily
rhymed 'Condy' and 'Hemings') chose to rename the play
after its monarch in their 1623 Folio collection.

Henry VIII (1613), 1.4:

SANDYS (*to* WOLSEY). The red wine first must rise
   In their fair cheeks, my lord; then we shall have 'em
   Talk us to silence.

ANNE BOLEYN.   You are a °merry gamester,
   My Lord Sandys.

SANDYS.　　　　　　　Yes, if I °make my play.
　　Here's to your ladyship — and pledge it, madam,
　　For 'tis to such a thing—

ANNE BOLEYN.　　　　　　You cannot show me.

SANDYS (to WOLSEY).
　　I told your grace they would talk anon.

　　　　　　　　Drum and trumpet. Chambers discharged.

WOLSEY.　　　　　　　　　　What's that?

CHAMBERLAIN. Look out there, some of ye.

WOLSEY.　　　　　　　　　　What warlike voice,
　　And to what end, is this?

from Anon., 'Upon the Pitiful Burning of the Globe
Playhouse' (1613):

　　This fearful fire began above,
　　　　A wonder strange and true,
　　And to the stage-house did remove,
　　　　As round as tailor's °clew;
　　And burnt down both beam and °snag,
　　And did not spare the silken flag.
　　　　O sorrow, pitiful sorrow,
　　　　And yet all this is true.

　　Out run the knights, out run the lords,
　　　　And there was great ado;
　　Some lost their hats, and some their swords,
　　　　Then out run Burbage too;
　　The reprobates, though drunk on Monday,
　　Pray'd for the Fool and Henry Condy.
　　　　O sorrow, pitiful sorrow,
　　　　And yet all this is true.

　　The periwigs and drum-heads fry,
　　　　Like to a °butter-firkin;
　　A woeful burning did betide
　　　　To many a good buff jerkin.
　　Then with swollen eyes, like drunken Flemings,

Distressèd stood old stuttering Hemings.
  O sorrow, pitiful sorrow,
  And yet all this is true.

'Where is he?'

'When my cue comes, call me and I will answer,' announces Bottom, on waking from his dreamy transformation into a donkey, and his even dreamier seduction by Titania, the Queen of Fairies. 'My next is "Most fair Pyramus". Heigh-ho! Peter Quince? Flute the bellows-mender? Snout the tinker? God's my life, stolen hence, and left me asleep?' (4.1). Meanwhile, Quince, Flute, Snout, and the rest of the mechnicals are chewing their fingernails as the time for 'curtain-up' looms. It is rather touching to notice how flustered Peter Quince is here: the author of *Pyramus and Thisbe* realizes that for all his previous arguments with him, without his 'difficult' lead-actor, his play will founder. But Bottom saves the day.

A Midsummer Night's Dream (1595), 4.2:

QUINCE. Have you sent to Bottom's house? Is he come home yet?

STARVELING. He cannot be heard of. Out of doubt he is °transported.

FLUTE. If he come not, then the play is marred, it goes not forward — doth it?

QUINCE. It is not possible. You have not a man in all Athens able to discharge Pyramus but he.

FLUTE. No, he hath simply the best wit of any handicraftman in Athens.

QUINCE. Yea, and the best °person too. And he is a very °paramour for a sweet voice.

FLUTE. You must say 'para*gon*': a 'pa*ramour*' is — God bless us — a thing of naught.

Enter SNUG *the joiner.*

SNUG. Masters, the Duke is coming from the temple, and there is two or three lords and ladies more, married. If our sport had gone forward, we had all been °made men.

FLUTE. O sweet °bully Bottom! Thus hath he lost sixpence a day during his life. He could not have °scaped sixpence a day. °An the Duke had not given him sixpence a day for playing Pyramus, I'll be hanged — he would have deserved it. Sixpence a day in Pyramus, or nothing.

Enter BOTTOM.

BOTTOM. Where are these lads! Where are these hearts!

QUINCE. Bottom? O most courageous day! O most happy hour!

BOTTOM. Masters, I am to discourse wonders — but ask me not what. For if I tell you, I am no true Athenian. I will tell you everything, right as it fell out.

QUINCE. Let us hear, sweet Bottom.

BOTTOM. Not a word of me.

6

Audiences, Critics, and Tours

Critics, avaunt! For you are fish of prey,
And feed, like sharks, upon an infant play.

William Congreve (1693)

1 ACTOR. If you see flaws, please,
   Don't drop your jaws, please,
   No loud guffaws, please,
   When actors enter late.

2 ACTOR. When there's a pause, please,
   Lots of applause, please,
   And we'd appreciate
   You turning off your cell phones while we wait.

Stephen Sondheim (2004)

Like all his fellow actors since, Shakespeare depended intensely on an audience's favourable reaction for his livelihood. Unlike most actors since, however, the audiences he observed from the stage ranged across the entire society through which he rose. Rather as their cast-lists broke all the rules by mingling Kings with Clowns, and Princes with Gravediggers, so Shakespeare's plays seem – almost miraculously – to have equally appealed to royal audiences at court, the lowly groundlings in the yards of the public theatres, the lords who attended both venues, and a growing critical intelligentsia. It was a precarious balancing-act to pull off – and one that several of Shakespeare's contemporaries seriously misjudged.

Complaints by the City authorities about the social 'inconvenience' of London's theatres began to be voiced more or less immediately following their construction, and regular demands were made for their closure. The protection afforded to the various companies by their aristocratic patrons, however, usually guaranteed their professional security. Even when plague shut down their theatres, as it periodically did throughout Shakespeare's working lifetime, actors could always revert to their original status as 'strolling players', and hit the road on the provincial tours that have been increasingly well documented in recent years.

Sometimes, however, it was a play (rather than plague) that did the damage. In 1597, for example, the production of a lost play called *The Isle of Dogs* resulted in imprisonment for one of its authors (Ben Jonson), permanent exile from London for another (Thomas Nashe), and the immediate closure – and threatened demolition – of *all* London's theatres. ('As Actaeon was worried by his own hounds,' commented the early theatre critic Francis Meres in 1598, 'so is Tom Nashe of his *Isle of Dogs*.') Eight years later, in September 1605, Jonson found himself staring at the walls of another prison-cell, following his arrest, along with co-authors John Marston and George Chapman, for ridiculing the Scots in *Eastward Ho!* (Jonson's mother later admitted that she was prepared to smuggle poison into his cell if the rumoured sentence of having 'their ears cut, and noses' had been carried out.) The Globe's greatest ever triumph – the nine succesive performances there of Thomas Middleton's *A Game at Chess* in August 1624 – resulted in a warrant for its author's arrest. (The play impertinently dramatized – and threatened to interfere with – contemporary international diplomacy with Spain.) And meanwhile Shakespeare himself had been severely compromised, when the followers of the Earl of Essex commissioned a revival of *Richard II* at the Globe on the eve of his abortive *coup d'état* in February 1601. Subsequent government interrogation of the company's spokesman, Augustine Phillips, defused the situation, and the crisis passed – as it had on these other occasions – but not without supplying a salutary reminder (if any were required) of the fragile ambivalence of the players' status. As a wealthy showbiz impresario simultaneously at the constant beck and call of his patrons, Shakespeare negotiated a strange double-life as master and servant – a double vision that surely animates the endless perspective of his plays. The production of *The Mousetrap* that Hamlet mounts for his uncle–King is tantamount to treason, after all.

The dazzling success of his career famously led Jonson to posthumous praise of 'our swan of Avon', and his poetic 'flights upon the banks of Thames, / That so did take Eliza, and our James'. The reality of Shakespeare's royal favour was somewhat less romantic. 'Sir,' wrote one of King James's bureaucrats in January 1605, 'I have sent – and been all this morning hunting – for players, jugglers, & such kind of creatures, but find them hard to find; wherefore, leaving notes for them to seek me, Burbage is come, and says there is no new play that the Queen hath not seen, but they have revived an old one called "Love's Labour Lost", which for wit & mirth he says will please her exceedingly. And this is appointed to be played tomorrow night.' (And that's an order.) Meanwhile there were other pressures. 'The theatre is your poets' Royal Exchange', declared Thomas Dekker in *The Gull's Horn Book* (1609), likening playwrights to so many merchants, who 'barter away that light commodity of words' for the sheer sound of applause ('the breath of the great beast', he calls it), but 'which, like the threatenings of two cowards, vanish all into air'. (Some poets' transactions were less ephemeral than others, of course, and the permanently impoverished Dekker always needed a decent agent.)

Simultaneously subject to the market forces of the public theatre and the delicate gauge of aristocratic favour, Shakespeare's 'place' in society was always more difficult to define in his lifetime than the measure of wealth he displayed in buying the Stratford mansion known as 'New Place' in 1597. However loudly old money must have sneered, it was the ephemeral sound of repeated applause – whether the polite smatter at court or the roar of the groundlings at the Globe – that continued to pay for it, and his ear was always finely tuned to its nuances. The following section seeks to demonstrate the range of those attentions.

The 'palpable hit' that nearly all Shakespeare's plays struck among both courtiers and groundlings has become a cliché of the 'judgement' of theatre criticism – despite the lethal duel to which it originally refers in *Hamlet*. 'Well!' concedes Laertes there, before resting, resuming position, and announcing the word all actors know (and dread): 'Again!'

On the road again

Whether because of plague, politics, or sheer accident, London's open-air theatres regularly 'went dark' during Shakespeare's career, requiring a resumption by their permanent companies of the hazards and slog of provincial touring – literally drumming up trade around the marketplace, and busking the grander effects of their better-rehearsed plays on the succession of temporary stages they commanded. Henslowe records a loan he made 'to the company [i.e. the Admiral's Men] to buy a drum when to go into the country' in February 1600. And when Parolles, in *All's Well That Ends Well* (1604), is interrogated about Bertram's military skills ('What say you to his expertness in war?'), his answer insultingly likens his friend's expertise to the make-believe of a different sort of 'troupe': 'Faith, sir, he's led the drum before the English tragedians' (4.3). Bands of 'strolling players' (the term is first recorded in a play by Richard Brome in 1641) repeatedly enter Shakespeare's stage, most famously, of course, in *Hamlet*. (It is intriguing that Polonius's praise for 'the best actors in the world' includes references to the two Roman playwrights to whom Shakespeare himself had recently been compared: 'As Plautus and Seneca are accounted the best for Comedy and Tragedy among the Latins; so Shakespeare among the English is the most excellent in both kinds for the stage'.)*

---

* Francis Meres, *Palladis Tamia: Wits Treasury* (1598). The Shakespeare plays that Meres goes on to praise famously include ('for Comedy') 'his *Love labours won*', a play known to have been printed by 1600 – so bequeathing to posterity the tantalizing possibility of the discovery in some dusty archive of a genuinely new Shakespeare play.

Hamlet (1600–1), 2.2:

POLONIUS. My lord, I have news to tell you.

HAMLET. My lord, I have news to tell you. When Roscius
was an actor in Rome —

POLONIUS. The actors are come hither, my lord.

HAMLET. °Buzz, buzz!

POLONIUS. Upon my honour —

HAMLET. °'Then came each actor on his ass —'

POLONIUS. The best actors in the world, either for
tragedy, comedy, history, pastoral, pastoral-comical,
historical-pastoral, tragical-historical, tragical-comical-
historical-pastoral, °scene individable or poem
unlimited: Seneca cannot be too heavy, nor Plautus too
light. For the law of writ and the liberty, these are the
only men.

A similar incursion supplies the climax to the comic subplot of
Thomas Middleton's *Hengist, King of Kent* (1620), in which the
self-important Mayor of Queenborough (the play's alternative
title) welcomes a troupe of players to perform at his house, and
so lend prestige to his office. In fact, though, as soon becomes
clear, they are a band of thieves and conmen, who 'only take
the name of country comedians to abuse simple people, with a
printed play or two they bought at Canterbury last week for
sixpence' – among them presumably a copy of *Hamlet*.

Thomas Middleton, *The Mayor of Queenborough* (1620), 5.1:

CLERK. Please your worship, here are a certain company
of players —

MAYOR. Ha, players?

CLERK. Country comedians, interluders, sir — desires your
worship's favour and leave to enact in the town hall.

MAYOR. I' th' town hall? 'Tis ten to one I never grant them
that. Call 'em before my worship. If my house will not

serve their turn, I would fain see the proudest he lend them a barn.

Enter a company of pretended PLAYERS.

Now, sirs, are you comedians?

1 PLAYER. We are anything, sir: comedians, tragedians, tragi-comedians, comi-tragedians, pastoralists, humorists, clownists, and satirists. We have 'em, sir, from the smile to the laugh, from the laugh to the handkerchief. [...]

MAYOR. But which is your merriest play? That I would hearken after.

1 PLAYER. Your worship shall hear their names, and take your choice.

Choosing the entertainment

Middleton's player/conman (for some the distinction has never been absolute) knowingly supplies a list of fictional play-titles (*Gull Upon Gull*, *Woodcock of Our Side*, *The Cheater and the Clown*) to the duped Mayor that tip us off to what is really going on (woodcocks being proverbially stupid and 'gullible' birds). The bill of fare offered by such touring companies earned repeated sarcasm from the playwrights whose new plays they often supplanted. Those listed by the 'gentleman scholar' playwright Master Posthaste, for example, in John Marston's *Histriomastix* (1599–1600), seem decidedly mismatched to their generic labels: '*Mother Gurton's Needle*: a tragedy. *The Devil and Dives*: a comedy. *A Russet Coat and a Knave's Cap*: an infernal...' (2.4). 'Pretty names,' replies Marston's Usher (presumably with a theatrical upward cast of his eyes).

The 'usher' (a word related to its demeaning twentieth-century demotion to 'usherette') was the household servant charged with liaising between a lord and his visitors, and therefore with organizing its entertainments – the same court official that Shakespeare named Philostrate in the first draft of

A Midsummer Night's Dream, who there presents to Duke Theseus a similarly ridiculous list. The first three proposals he reports are superbly inappropriate to a marriage: the attempted rape and fatal brawl at the wedding-feast of Pirithous ('The Battle of the Centaurs'); the violent dismemberment of the poet Orpheus ('The Riot of the Tipsy Bacchanals'); and the scornful accusation of an aristocratic patron's neglect ('Mourning for the Death of Learning'). *Pyramus and Thisbe* must have seemed the best of a bad lot. Shakespeare at some point returned to the scene, reassigning Philostrate's lines to Egeus, and redistributing what was originally a long speech by Theseus into a punchier dialogue between him and Lysander. The following is from that revised text.

A Midsummer Night's Dream (1595), 5.1:

THESEUS. Call Egeus.

EGEUS.   Here, mighty Theseus.

THESEUS. Say, what °abridgement have you for this evening?
    What masque? What music? How shall we beguile
    The lazy time, if not with some delight?

EGEUS. There is a °brief how many sports are °ripe:
    Make choice of which your highness will see first.

                              LYSANDER *reads a paper.*

LYSANDER. 'The Battle with the Centaurs, to be sung
    By an Athenian eunuch to the harp'?

THESEUS. We'll none of that. That have I told my love
    In glory of my kinsman °Hercules.

LYSANDER. 'The Riot of the Tipsy Bacchanals,
    Tearing the Thracian Singer in their Rage'?

THESEUS. That is an old °device, and it was play'd
    When I from Thebes came last a conqueror.

LYSANDER. 'The Thrice-Three Muses, Mourning for the
    Death
    Of Learning, Late Deceas'd in Beggary'?

THESEUS. That is some satire keen and critical,
  Not sorting with a nuptial ceremony.

LYSANDER. 'A Tedious Brief Scene of Young Pyramus
  And his Love Thisbe: very tragical mirth'?

THESEUS. Merry *and* 'tragical'? 'Tedious' *and* 'brief?
  That is hot ice and wondrous strange snow!
  How shall we find the °concord of this discord?

EGEUS. A play there is, my lord, some ten words long,
  Which is as 'brief' as I have known a play;
  But by ten words, my lord, it is too long,
  Which makes it 'tedious', for in all the play
  There is not one word apt, one player fitted.
  And 'tragical', my noble lord, it is,
  For Pyramus therein doth kill himself —
  Which when I saw rehears'd, I must confess,
  Made mine eyes water; but more merry tears
  The passion of loud laughter never shed.

THESEUS. What are they that do play it?

EGEUS. Hard-handed men that work in Athens here,
  Which never labour'd in their minds till now;
  And now have toil'd their °unbreath'd memories
  With this same play against your °nuptial.

THESEUS. And we will hear it.

Special instructions

What may be Shakespeare's earliest play begins with another visit to an aristocratic country house by a troupe of players, whose lord (like Hamlet, later) retains vivid memories of their last visit; and who (like Hamlet again) issues some special instructions, in this case to overlook the potentially eccentric behaviour of an important member of the audience who is a novice to theatre – and is, in fact, the drunken tinker Christopher Sly.

The Taming of the Shrew (1592), Induction, Scene 1:

LORD. How now? Who is it?

SERVANT.   An't please your honour, players
  That offer service to your lordship.

LORD. Bid them come near.

  Enter PLAYERS.

  Now, fellows, you are welcome.

PLAYERS. We thank your honour.

LORD. Do you intend to stay with me tonight?

1 PLAYER. So please your lordship to accept our duty.

LORD. With all my heart. This fellow I remember
  Since once he play'd a farmer's eldest son —
  'Twas where you woo'd the gentlewoman so well.
  I have forgot your name but, sure, that part
  Was aptly fitted and naturally perform'd.

2 PLAYER. I think 'twas °Soto that your honour means.

LORD. 'Tis very true, thou didst it excellent.
  Well, you are come to me in a happy time,
  The rather for I have some sport in hand
  Wherein your cunning can assist me much.
  There is a lord will hear you play tonight;
  But I am doubtful of your °modesties
  Lest °over-eyeing of his odd behaviour —
  For yet his honour never heard a play —
  You break into some merry passion
  And so offend him; for I tell you, sirs,
  If you should smile, he grows impatient.

1 PLAYER. Fear not, my lord, we can contain ourselves,
  Were he the °veriest antic in the world.

LORD. Go, sirrah, take them to the buttery,
  And give them friendly welcome every one.
  Let them want nothing that my house affords.

                            Exit SERVANT *with the* PLAYERS.

The watcher watched

The use to which Shakespeare has Hamlet put the arrival of the strolling players promotes their status from the comic fringes to the tragic core of his play. Shakespeare's great fan Thomas Heywood later supplied a fascinating precedent for Hamlet's device: perhaps they both 'heard' the same report.

Hamlet (1600–1), 2.2:

HAMLET.   I have heard
   That guilty creatures sitting at a play
   Have by the very cunning of the scene
   Been struck so to the soul that presently
   They have proclaim'd their malefactions;
   For murder, though it have no tongue, will speak
   With most miraculous °organ. I'll have these players
   Play something like the murder of my father
   Before mine uncle. I'll observe his looks;
   I'll °tent him to the quick: if he but blench,
   I know my course. The spirit that I have seen
   May be the devil: and the devil hath power
   To assume a pleasing shape; yea, and perhaps
   Out of my weakness and my melancholy,
   As he is very potent with such spirits,
   Abuses me to damn me. I'll have grounds
   More °relative than this: the play's the thing
   Wherein I'll catch the conscience of the King.

from Thomas Heywood, *An Apology for Actors* (1612):

At Lynn in Norfolk, the then Earl of Sussex's players acting the old *History of Friar Francis*, and presenting a woman who [...] secretly murdered her husband, whose ghost haunted her, and at divers times in her most solitary and private contemplations, in most horrid and fearful shapes, appeared and stood before her: as this was acted, a townswoman (till then of good estimation and report), finding her conscience at this presentment extremely troubled, suddenly screeched and cried out, 'Oh my husband, my husband! I see the ghost of my husband fiercely threatening and menacing me!' At which shrill and unexpected outcry, the people about her, moved to a strange amazement, enquired the reason of her clamour, when presently un-urged she told them that seven years ago she [...] had poisoned her husband, whose fearful image personated itself in the shape of that ghost. Whereupon the murderess was apprehended, before the Justices further examined, and by her voluntary confession after condemned. That this is true, as well by the report of the actors as the records of the town, there are many eye-witnesses of this accident yet living vocally to confirm it.

Audience participation

The interplay between real life and performed fiction was a favourite device of Shakespeare's stage, from Hieronymo's scheme in Kyd's *Spanish Tragedy*, by which this alternative Master of the Revels casts the villainous members of the court in a play whose performance results in their actual onstage murders, via Hamlet's *Mousetrap*, to the later masques at King James's court that featured actual courtiers among their cast.

Thomas Kyd, *The Spanish Tragedy* (c. 1587), 4.1:

HIERONYMO. When in Toledo there I studièd,
    It was my chance to write a tragedy —
    See here, my lords —

                                    He shows them a book.

    Which long forgot, I found this other day.
    Now would your lordships favour me so much
    As but to grace me with your acting it,
    I mean each one of you to play a part. [...]
    I'll play the murderer, I warrant you,

For I already have conceited that.

BALTHAZAR. And what shall I?

HIERONYMO. Great Soliman the Turkish Emperor.

LORENZO. And I?

HIERONYMO. Erastus the knight of Rhodes.

BEL-IMPERIA. And I?

HIERONYMO. Perseda, chaste and resolute.
    And here, my lords, are several abstracts drawn,
    For each of you to note your parts,
    And act it as occasion's offer'd you. —
    You must provide a Turkish cap,
    A black moustachio and a °falchion —
    You with a cross like to a knight of Rhodes —
    And, madam, you must attire yourself
    Like °Phoebe, Flora, or the Huntress,
    Which to your discretion shall seem best.

'If you think I'm drunk, wait till you see the Duke of Buckingham'*

It seems that touring players were inured to the foibles of their aristocratic audiences – not least when a court masque to celebrate the King of Denmark's state visit in 1606 descended into chaos after too much drinking among the cast and audience. King James apparently seized the opportunity of the first upset to escape and pass out, leaving his brother-in-law King Christian to the mercies of the Three Graces.

Sir John Harington, July 1606

    The lady who did play the Queen [of Sheba]'s part did carry most precious gifts to both their majesties; but forgetting a rising to the canopy, overset her caskets

---

* The apocryphal riposte to a heckler in the stalls by the lubricated lead in a production of *Richard III*.

[of jelly and cream] into his Danish majesty's lap, and fell at his feet, though I rather think it was in his face. Much was the hurry and confusion; cloths and napkins were at hand to make all clean. [...] The entertainment and show went forward, and most of the presenters went backward or fell down, wine did so occupy their upper chambers. Now did appear in rich dress, Hope, Faith, and Charity. Hope did assay to speak, but wine did render her endeavours so feeble that she withdrew. Faith was then all alone, for I am certain she was not joined with good works, and left the court in a staggering condition. Charity came to the King's feet, and seemed to cover the multitude of sins her sisters had committed: in some sort she made obeisance, and brought gifts. [...] She then returned to Hope and Faith, who were both sick and spewing in the hall.

The suspension of disbelief

It is probably nothing more than an ironic coincidence that Shakespeare seems to have abandoned Hamlet's first-Act disquisition on the notorious drunkenness of the Danes ('They clepe us drunkards, and with swinish phrase / Soil our addition...'), a sequence cut from the Folio's theatre-based text. To actors of Shakespeare's generation, however, coping with the drunken King Claudius – or the drunken tinker Christopher Sly – went with the territory, and was all in a day's work.

from the Induction to Act Four, *The Taming of a Shrew* (1590):

DUKE (*onstage*). 'Peace, villain! Lay hands on them,
    And send them to prison straight.'

> *The stage empties, then* SLY *speaks from the audience.*

SLY. I say we'll have no sending to prison!

LORD. My lord, this is but the play — they're but in jest.

SLY. I tell thee, Sim, we'll have no sending to prison, that's flat. Why, Sim, am not I Don Christofero? Therefore I say they shall not go to prison.

LORD. No more they shall not, my lord — they be run away.

SLY. Are they run away, Sim? That's well. Then gi's some more drink, and let them play again.

LORD. Here, my lord.

SLY drinks, and then falls asleep.

Swapping roles

Whether because of the circular embrace of London's earliest public theatres, the convivial inn-yards that preceded them, or the variously crowded formal halls that supplied a constant round of alternative venues, Shakespeare's drama was always responsive to the presence of its audience, and the spirit of improvisation it provoked. That intimate sense is nowhere more beautifully caught than in the first of the Falstaff plays, where the Fat Knight and the reprobate Prince playfully impersonate, from the slangy perspective of the mid-1590s, the central characters of their own history play.

Henry IV, Part One (1596), 2.4:

PRINCE HAL. Do thou stand for my father and examine me upon the particulars of my life.

FALSTAFF. Shall I? °Content. This chair shall be my °state, this dagger my sceptre, and this cushion my crown.

PRINCE HAL. Thy state is taken for a °joint-stool, thy golden sceptre for a leaden dagger, and thy precious rich crown for a pitiful °bald crown.

FALSTAFF. Well, °an the °fire of grace be not quite out of thee, now shalt thou be moved. Give me a cup of °sack to make my eyes look red, that it may be thought I have wept, for I must speak in passion, and I will do it in King °Cambyses' vein.

PRINCE HAL (*bowing*). Well, here is my leg.

FALSTAFF. And here is my speech. (*As King Henry.*) 'Stand aside, nobility.'

HOSTESS. O Jesu, this is excellent sport, i'faith!

FALSTAFF. 'Weep not, sweet Queen, for trickling tears are vain.'

HOSTESS. O the Father, how he °holds his countenance!

FALSTAFF. 'For God's sake, lords, convey my °tristful Queen,

For tears do stop the floodgates of her eyes —'

HOSTESS. O Jesu, he doth it as like one of these °harlotry players as ever I see!

FALSTAFF. Peace, good pint-pot! Peace, good °tickle-brain! — 'Harry, I do not only marvel where thou spendest thy time, but also how thou art accompanied. For though the °camomile, the more it is trodden on the fast it grows, so youth, the more it is wasted the sooner it wears. […] For, Harry, now I do not speak to thee in drink but in tears, not in pleasure but in passion, not in words only but in woes also. And yet there is a virtuous man whom I have often noted in thy company, but I know not his name.'

PRINCE HAL. What manner of man, an it like your majesty?

FALSTAFF (*as King Henry*). 'A goodly, portly man, i'faith, and a corpulent; of a cheerful look, a pleasing eye, and a most noble carriage; and, as I think, his age some fifty or — by'r Lady! — inclining to three-score. And now I remember me: his name is Falstaff. […] Him keep with; the rest banish. And tell me now, thou naughty varlet, tell me, where hast thou been this month?'

PRINCE HAL. Dost thou speak like a king? Do thou stand for me, and I'll play my father.

FALSTAFF. Depose me?

'Shall I have audience?'

Mistress Quickly's appreciation of Falstaff's performance is so vociferous as to interrupt his performance ('Peace, good pint-pot!') and sponsor an improvised response – a piece of audience interaction that anticipates the climax of Hamlet's *Mousetrap*. We have already heard Hamlet's strenuous deprecation of the ill-disciplined Clown whose ad-libbed routines upstage the action by provoking 'some quantity of barren spectators to laugh too' (see above p. 51) – a slightly odd instruction, since it is hard to see quite what role the company Clown could play in *The Murder of Gonzago*. (Something like the Gravedigger in *Hamlet*, presumably, though we will never know, given that the performance is abandoned midway through.) The force of his criticism remains pertinent, however, and we probably all remember the irritation of witnessing a cheap laugh spreading through an audience, milked beyond its merit by the comedian responsible, and delaying the resumption of what Hamlet calls 'some necessary question of the play'. Still, better – at least from Shakespeare's point of view – to hear at such close quarters an audience's laughter than the 'hiss' of its disapproval. After all, even 'a good play', as the theatregoer Francis Meres observed in 1598, 'sometimes is hissed off the stage, through the fault of the player ill acting it,' and Shakespeare's ear was keenly attuned to the range of such human music. It is an accident of history that the only contemporary drawing of an Elizabethan playhouse – the de Witt sketch of the Swan (see above, p. 113) – leaves out the central feature that brought such 'wooden Os' into bustling, noisy, and no doubt smelly life: the audience. Thomas Platter paid slightly more attention to them during his visit to the Globe to see *Julius Caesar* in September 1599.

from Thomas Platter's *Travels* (1604), from the German:

Thus daily at two in the afternoon, London has two, sometimes three plays running in different places, competing with each other, and those which play best obtain most spectators. The playhouses are so constructed that they play on a raised platform, so that everyone has a good view. There are different galleries and places, however, where the seating is better and more comfortable and therefore more expensive. For whoever cares to stand below only pays one English penny, but if he wishes to sit he enters by another door, and pays another penny, while if he desires to sit in the most comfortable seats, which are cushioned, where he not only sees everything well but can also be seen, then he pays another English penny at another door. And during the performance food and drink are carried round the audience, so that for what one cares to pay one may also have refreshment.

From a rustle to a hiss

Whether in rapt attention or loud acclaim, bemused silence or audible disapproval, Shakespeare's audiences supplied a constant accompaniment to the plays he acted in, and repeatedly featured in the imaginative life of his plays – as the following extracts reveal. The speaker of his Sonnet 110 may regret making himself 'a motley to the view' (see p. 118), but it is the 'noise' associated with doing so that caught his attention – as for example the following description of Queen Anne Boleyn's coronation, shortly after its spectacular recreation had, hopefully, prompted a similar response on the stage of the Globe.

Henry VIII (1613), 4.1:

3 GENTLEMAN. Believe me, sir, she is the goodliest woman
    That ever lay by man; which when the people
    Had the full view of, such a noise arose
    As the °shrouds make at sea in a stiff tempest,
    As loud, and to as many tunes: hats, cloaks —
    Doublets, I think — flew up; and had their faces
    Been loose, this day they had been lost. Such joy
    I never saw before.

When Bassanio correctly chooses the third casket in *The Merchant of Venice* (below), and so wins the hand of the beautiful heiress Portia, his train of bewildered and joyful thought includes two separate references to an audience's reaction. The first likens his success in the competition to a sportsman's victory in the ring ('contending in a prize'), momentarily dizzied by the applause he hears; the second likens his own tongue-tied reaction in the face of Portia's declaration of love to the quiet bustle of cautiously deferential approval commanded by a powerful speech. Both images were wholly in keeping with the stages where they were first voiced. London's theatres frequently doubled as the rings for fencing matches (known as 'playing a prize') of the sort dramatized at the end of *Hamlet* (and perhaps also wrestling bouts of the kind that initiates the action of *As You Like It*); while the thoughtful murmurs sponsored by an impressive speech were becoming familiar noises during Shakespeare's plays.

The Merchant of Venice (1596–7), 3.2:

BASSANIO. A gentle scroll! Fair lady, by your leave,
  I come by note to give, and to receive.
  Like one of two contending in a prize
  That thinks he hath done well in people's eyes,
  Hearing applause and universal shout,
  Giddy in spirit, still gazing in a doubt
  Whether those peals of praise be his or no —
  So, thrice-fair lady, stand I even so,
  As doubtful whether what I see be true,
  Until confirm'd, sign'd, ratified by you.

PORTIA. You see me, Lord Bassanio, where I stand,
  Such as I am. [...]

BASSANIO. Madam, you have bereft me of all words;
  Only my blood speaks to you in my veins,
  And there is such confusion in my powers
  As after some oration fairly spoke
  By a belovèd prince there doth appear
  Among the buzzing pleasèd multitude,

Where every something being blent together
Turns to a wild of nothing, save of joy
Express'd, and not express'd.

'Do not consent / That Antony speak in his funeral,' cautions
that consummate politician Cassius in the immediate after-
math of Julius Caesar's assassination, but Brutus overrules his
friend's advice, honourably – but disastrously – granting Mark
Antony the second slot from 'the same pulpit whereto I am
going, / After my speech is ended' (3.1). Brutus's speech to the
people is in worthy prose ('Romans, countrymen, and lovers,
hear me for my cause and be silent, that you may hear'); Mark
Antony delivers his in a glorious blank verse that is still famous
today ('Friends, Romans, countrymen, lend me your ears!').
Shakespeare's King Richard II, faced with Bolingbroke's pop-
ularity, has the opposite problem – according to his uncle, the
Duke of York – and one all-too familiar to the actors who first
performed the play: how to cap a star-turn.

Richard II (1595), 5.2:

DUKE. You would have thought the very windows spake,
　　So many greedy looks of young and old
　　Through °casements darted their desiring eyes
　　Upon his visage, and that all the walls
　　With painted imagery had said at once,
　　'Jesu preserve thee! Welcome, Bolingbroke!',
　　Whilst he, from the one side to the other turning,
　　Bare-headed, lower than his proud steed's neck,
　　Bespake them thus: 'I thank you, countrymen,'
　　And thus still doing, thus he pass'd along.

DUCHESS. Alack, poor Richard! Where rode he the whilst?

DUKE. As in a theatre the eyes of men,
　　After a well-grac'd actor leaves the stage,
　　Are idly bent on him that enters next,
　　Thinking his prattle to be tedious,
　　Even so, or with much more contempt, men's eyes
　　Did scowl on Richard. No man cried God save him!

Shakespeare's description of the eager glances 'darted' from the clustered windows and decorated walls of London's narrow medieval streets must have gained vivid force from the bobbing heads and peering eyes to be seen in the galleries of the theatres where it played. A similar double perspective accompanies a marvellous passage in a play later performed at the Fortune in Clerkenwell – a square playhouse, otherwise 'contrived and fashioned like unto' the Globe, and by the same architect – in which a wealthy aristocrat's proud display of his picture galleries melds into a description of the theatre where the speech first played.

Thomas Middleton and Thomas Dekker, *The Roaring Girl* (1611), 1.2:

SIR ALEXANDER. The furniture that doth adorn this room
    Cost many a fair grey °groat ere it came here;
    But good things are most cheap when they're most dear.
    Nay, when you look into my galleries —
    How °bravely they are trimm'd up — you all shall swear
    You're highly pleas'd to see what's set down there:
    Stories of men and women, mix'd together,
    Fair ones with foul, like sunshine in wet weather.
    Within one square a thousand heads are laid
    So close that all of heads the room seems to be made;
    As many faces there, fill'd with blithe looks,
    Show like the promising titles of new books
    Writ merrily, the readers being their own eyes,
    Which seem to move and to give °plaudities;
    And here and there, whilst with obsequious ears
    Throng'd heaps do listen, a cutpurse thrusts and leers
    With hawk's eyes for his prey — I need not show him:
    By a hanging villainous look yourselves may know him,
    The face is drawn so °rarely. Then, sir, below,
    The very floor, as 'twere, waves to and fro,
    And, like a floating island, seems to move
    Upon a sea bound in with shores above.

Middleton likens the floor of the Fortune's yard, with its hundreds of bobbing heads, to the sea, and its thrust stage to an island – thus continuing in distant Clerkenwell the maritime imagery familiar from the Bankside theatres (see above, p. 12). The milling crowds of such a full house were notorious for the easy pickings of the cutpurse ('At plays,' wrote Robert Greene, 'the nip [pickpocket] standeth there leaning… against the door as men go in,' clocking 'what every man hath in his purse, & where, in what place, and in which sleeve or pocket'). Audiences were also notorious – not necessarily accurately – for the alleged promiscuity of their female members, a context that lends a grim *frisson* to Leontes's deranged suspicions of cuckoldry in *The Winter's Tale*, where his lubricious insinuations startlingly implicate the audience at the Globe. (The queasy imagery of a fish-pond raided by a neighbouring poacher may have struck another chord, since the Globe itself was closely neighboured on Bankside by the fish farms known as the Pike Gardens.)

The Winter's Tale (1610), 1.2:

LEONTES. Go play, boy, play. — Thy mother plays, and I
    Play too; but so disgrac'd a part, whose issue
    Will hiss me to my grave, contempt and clamour
    Will be my °knell. Go play, boy, play. There have been
    (Or I am much deceiv'd) cuckolds ere now,
    And many a man there is (even at this present,
    Now, while I speak this) holds his wife by th'arm
    That little thinks she has been sluic'd in's absence,
    And his pond fish'd by his next neighbour; by
    Sir Smile, his neighbour.

Such 'metatheatrical' effects, of course, are prompted by Leontes's conversation with, and dismissal of, his little son Mamillius, over whose head (literally) the soliloquy is addressed, and whose childish 'play' cues the theatrical sense of that word (his doubly imagined 'part' is that of a cuckold) – the shame of which, he says, will elicit lifelong hissing from this theatre of the world. In fact, the effect of his speech must first have been more akin to the rustling 'confusion' Bassanio describes (see above, p. 162) than the 'hissing snakes' that so often killed off and buried a new play. (Reviews could 'sting', even then.) The following, slightly later, description by William Fennor, suggests that rounds of hissing – like the rounds of ill-disciplined laughter that Hamlet had condemned – were sometimes contagiously 'set on' among 'barren spectators'.

from William Fennor, *Fennors Descriptions* (1616):

> They °screw'd their scurvy jaws and look'd awry,
> Like hissing snakes adjudging it to die,
> When wits of gentry did applaud the same
> With silver shouts of high loud-sounding fame,
> Whilst under-standing grounded men contemn'd it
> And, wanting wit (like fools to judge), condemn'd it.
> Clapping, or hissing, is the only mean
> That tries and searches out a well-writ Scene:
> So it is thought by Ignoramus' crew,
> But that good wits acknowledge as untrue;
> The stinkards oft will hiss without a cause,
> And for a bawdy jest will give applause.
> Let one but ask the reason why they roar,
> They'll answer: ''Cause the rest did so before.'

Heckling

Sometimes, however, it was the 'wits of gentry' that were ignorant. When Holofernes's pageant of the Worthies in *Love's Labour's Lost* grinds to a halt in the face of the heckling ridicule of its gentlemen spectators, Armado's rebuke from the stage carries a quietly chilling dignity. 'The sweet war-man is dead and rotten,' he reminds them, stepping out of his character as Hector of Troy: 'When he breathed, he was a man' (5.2). And for all that the rehearsals of *Pyramus and Thisbe* have amused us, the mockery Starveling receives in performance affords a momentarily vivid glimpse of an actor's exasperation. It is always easy to mock or criticize (in this case an extended riff on the prop the thin figure of Starveling carries as Moonshine); it is more polite – and ultimately more rewarding – to suspend one's disbelief.

A Midsummer Night's Dream (1595), 5.1:

STARVELING (*as Moonshine*).
　　'This lantern doth the hornèd moon present—'

DEMETRIUS. He should have worn the horns on his head.

THESEUS. He is no crescent, and his horns are invisible within the circumference.

STARVELING (*as Moonshine*).
　　'This lantern doth the hornèd moon present,
　　Myself the man i' th' moon do seem to be—'

THESEUS. This is the greatest error of all the rest: the man should be put into the lantern. How is it else the man i' th' moon?

DEMETRIUS. He dares not come there for the candle, for you see it is already °in snuff.

HIPPOLYTA. I am aweary of this moon. Would he would change!

THESEUS. It appears by his small light of discretion that he is in the wane; but yet in courtesy, in all reason, we must stay the time.

LYSANDER. Proceed, Moon.

STARVELING. All I have to say is to tell you that the lantern is the moon, I am the man i' th' moon, this thorn-bush my thorn-bush, and this dog my dog.

One early admirer of *Love's Labour's Lost* was George Chapman, who adapted the conceit of a boorishly interrupted recital (see above, p. 130) by getting his retaliation in first. In the following exchange, an innkeeper, Verone, has written a speech of welcome to the King and Queen and their retinue, to be spoken by his son, which simultaneously mocks and praises their quality.

George Chapman, *An Humorous Day's Mirth* (1597), scene 13:

BOY. 'Fair ladies most tender
     And nobles most slender,
     And gentles whose wits be scarce —'

KING. My host, why do you call us 'nobles most slender'?

VERONE. °An it shall please your grace, to be slender is to be proper, and therefore where my boy says 'nobles most slender', it is as much to say 'fine and proper nobles'.

LEMOT. Yea, but why do you call us 'gentles whose wits be scarce'?

VERONE. To be scarce is to be rare, and therefore, whereas he says 'gentles whose wits be scarce', is as much as to say 'gentles whose wits be rare'.

LEMOT (*to the* BOY). Well, forwards, °truchman.

BOY. 'Fair ladies most tender
     And nobles most slender,
     And gentles whose wits be scarce,
     Queen Fortune doth come
     With her trump and her drum,
     As it may appear by my verse —'

LABESHA (*to* VERONE). Come hither. Are you a schoolmaster? Where was Fortune 'queen'? Of what country or kingdom? [...]

VERONE (*to the* KING). I'll alter it, if it please your grace.

KING. No, 'tis very well.

BOY. Father, I must begin again. They interrupt me so.

Two views from the stalls

Fennor's punning contempt for the critical understanding of the 'under-standing' groundlings (above, p. 166) presents a split between inferior populist taste and the higher-minded opinions of the 'gentry' that remains with us to this day (between Agatha Christie's *Mousetrap*, say, and the latest *Hamlet*) – one of the many abiding legacies of Elizabethan theatre architecture. Shakespeare's plays (with one or two exceptions) somehow managed to appeal to all tiers of his audience. Hamlet, the student prince, may priggishly deprecate the mugging Clown in Act Two, but his later eulogy over Yorick's skull feels like an emotional graduation. It is also interesting that the austerely intellectual Cassius is first and foremost described as someone who 'loves no plays'.

Julius Caesar (1599), 1.2:

CAESAR. I do not know the man I should avoid
   So soon as that spare Cassius. He reads much,
   He is a great observer, and he looks
   Quite through the deeds of men. He loves no plays
   As thou dost, Antony; he hears no music.
   Seldom he smiles, and smiles in such a sort
   As if he mock'd himself and scorn'd his spirit
   That could be mov'd to smile at anything.

We may perhaps recognize the quality of that knowingly sceptical smile, whether on the faces of the academic participants of modern 'Bardbiz' ('Here we go again,' I remember a professor once sighing to me as the lights dimmed on a new production of *Hamlet*), or those of the fidgeting recipients of corporate hospitality. But if the spectacle of such a bland reaction might irk an actor-playwright from the stage, this is as nothing to the fury levelled nowadays at an audience's fits of coughing ('an act of aggression', according to Harold Pinter), and the beeps and tinkles of their mobile phones. Elizabethan theatregoers had to face separate irritations (among other things, the stink of tobacco), but none more virulently expressed than in the following poem by John Weever, apparently inspired by finding himself seated next to a snuffly and over-perfumed old (*'vetulam'*) lady at the Rose or Globe.

John Weever, 'In Eripham vetulam', *Epigrammes* (1599)

°Eripha, that old trot, every day
Wafts o'er the water for to see a play,
And there a wither'd o'er-worn face she shows
Beset with rubies, and stopp'd full of ooze.
This water-witch a patch hath for th' rheum,
Her carcase she with aloes doth perfume,
With musk, civet, oliban, myrrh, incense,
Breathing out an aromatic redolence:
Her foulness makes me oft mine eyes up close,
Her sweetness makes me wish I were all nose.

Three notices

As often as not, however, it was the new play that stank, and the 'notices' supplied by its first audiences were closely monitored, sometimes resulting in a revised script for its second performance. Shakespeare presents a range of critical responses to the strolling players he depicts in his plays – often from a husband-and-wife team of critics. The bewildered Christopher Sly pretends to have enjoyed the play in order to retire to bed with his wife (in fact a page-boy cast in the role); Duke Theseus gently rebukes his bride for her dismissive judgement of the mechanicals' hopelessly optimistic performance of *Pyramus and Thisbe*; and Queen Gertrude is one of the first to notice her husband's discomfort at *The Mousetrap*.

The Taming of the Shrew (1592), 1.1:

> *The Presenters above speak.*

1 SERVANT. My lord, you nod: you do not mind the play.

SLY. Yes, by Saint Anne I do. A good matter, surely. Comes there any more of it?

PAGE-BOY (*as Sly's wife*). My lord, 'tis just begun.

SLY. 'Tis a very excellent piece of work, madam lady.
(*Aside.*) Would 'twere done!

They sit and °mark.

A Midsummer Night's Dream (1595), 5.1:

HIPPOLYTA. This is the silliest stuff that e'er I heard.

THESEUS. The best in this kind are but shadows, and the
worst are no worse if imagination amend them.

HIPPOLYTA. It must be your imagination, then, and not
theirs.

THESEUS. If we imagine no worse of them than they of
themselves, they may pass for excellent men.

Hamlet (1600–1), 3.2:

LUCIANUS.
'Thoughts black, hands apt, drugs fit, and time agreeing,
°Confederate season, else no creature seeing,
Thou mixture rank, of midnight weeds collected,
With Hecate's bane thrice blasted, thrice infected,
Thy natural magic and dire property
On wholesome life usurps immediately.'

He pours the poison in the sleeping King's ears.

HAMLET. He poisons him i' th' garden for his estate. His
name's Gonzago. The story is extant, and written in
very choice Italian. You shall see anon how the
murderer gets the love of Gonzago's wife —

OPHELIA. The King rises.

HAMLET. What, °frighted with false fire?

QUEEN. How fares my lord?

POLONIUS. °Give o'er the play.

KING. Give me some light. Away!

POLONIUS. Lights, lights, lights!

Epilogues and Afterlives

The play is done; the curtain drops,
  Slow falling to the prompter's bell.
A moment yet the actor stops,
  And looks around to say farewell.

William Makepeace Thackeray (1848)

What is our life? A play of passion,
Our mirth the music of division;
Our mothers' wombs the tiring-houses be,
Where we are dress'd for this short comedy;
Heaven the judicious sharp spectator is
That sits and marks still who doth act amiss;
Our graves that hide us from the searching sun
Are like drawn curtains when the play is done.
Thus march we playing to our °latest rest:
Only we die in earnest, that's no jest.

Sir Walter Ralegh (c. 1614)

After their hardwon command of an audience's attention at the beginning of their plays, dramatists of Shakespeare's generation faced the opposite problem in finding ways to signal their ending, whether after (public) open-air or (private) candle-lit performances. Modern practitioners have a wide range of resources at their disposal to cue applause and dispersal, from the old-fashioned 'Curtain', via the simple 'Blackout' or 'Slow Fade', to the less subtle operation of 'House Lights' – or the still starker screen that the Monty Python team used to project after curtain-call at their concerts, initially featuring the words 'The End', and then, in flashing letters, 'Piss Off'. Their Jacobethan counterparts matched that range. The manuscript 'platts' and prompt-books of their plays, and the printed texts eventually made from them, all displayed a prominent 'FINIS' at the end for the benefit of their readers. 'The End' is an impossible stage-direction to perform. *'Exeunt omnes'* is more practical, of course, but the mere clearing of the stage can never prevent an audience anticipating a further scene. Hence that tentative embarrassment about applause that, despite the best efforts of lighting-designers, continues to afflict the end of modern productions, even of classics with famous last lines.

One of the simplest technical tools at Shakespeare's disposal to counter-act this uncertainty was therefore the rhyming couplet. 'For never was a story of more woe,' concludes the Prince of Verona, 'Than this of Juliet and her Romeo': the sense of closure is unmissable, as much for the rhyme and rhythm of his words as for their content. In the days when plays were 'through-run', however, with no formal scene-breaks dividing them, rhyming couplets also served the purpose of clearing the emotional ground between one scene and the next, prompting in audiences as much expectation of a new mood to come as drawing a final line under the events they have witnessed. And meanwhile, of course, Shakespeare often deliberately broke the conventions. Fortinbras's great final speech in *Hamlet* gravitates to a couplet ('Such a sight as this / Becomes the field, but here shows much amiss'), but then interrupts his audiences' gathering sense that applause is wanted by appending the half-line of its famous last words – 'Go, bid the soldiers shoot' – as if to leave dangling the same foreboding at the end of the play as at its beginning ('Who's there?'). Such poetic sophistication aside, the practicalities of stage business in any case demanded a clearer signal to audiences that that was their lot. And so, *'Enter the Epilogue'*.

As unambiguous as a modern blackout followed by house lights, the device of the Epilogue was the most obvious means by which to return a play's passengers from its 'dream of passion' to the everyday world. Like the Prologues and Choruses that often announced and punctuated their action – and like them, often tailored to a specific performance – a play's Epilogue blurred the distinction between actor, author, and role, reversing the Prologue's earlier manoeuvre from real life to fiction. Performances at court, in particular, often took the opportunity to supply an appropriately gracious bow in the form of an Epilogue specifically tailored to the occasion. ('Your Majesty hath seen the play,' begins Ben Jonson's Epilogue to *Bartholomew Fair* on 1 November 1614, before King James; 'It is our fear (dread sovereign) we have been / Too tedious,' crawls Heywood's Epilogue to a revival of *The Jew of Malta* before King Charles in 1633.) At the public theatres, however, an Epilogue's cue for applause prompted a further round of entertainment in the form of a dance by the entire company. The penultimate word (before 'FINIS') in all early printed texts of *Much Ado About Nothing*, for example, is not '*Exeunt*' but '*Dance*', and one eye-witness report from the Globe in September 1599 corroborates the convention: 'At the end of the play, they danced together admirably and exceedingly gracefully, according to their custom, two in each group dressed in men's and women's apparel.'

Remarkably, the author of those words was Thomas Platter, and the play capped by this dance was Shakespeare's *Julius Caesar* – surely among the remotest in tone or plot from such frivolity. But if the change in gear seems crashing to modern sensibilities, it is partly because we have lost the all but magical sense with which our Elizabethan forebears regarded music: 'the best comforter / To an unsettled fancy', as Prospero calls it (*The Tempest*, 5.1). The group rhythm of such a dance after *Julius Caesar* may therefore have served a suitably double purpose at the first Globe, at once restoring cosmic harmony to the fractured world the play depicts around its mock-Roman pillars, and preparing the mass of its temporary extras in the auditorium to clear off.

Music of some sort or another seems always to have rounded off an afternoon's theatregoing, one eyewitness describing the throng 'at the playhouse doors, / When ended is the play, the dance, and song'. Whether that final song was the traditionally bawdy Jig of the Clown or a more artful lyrical performance (see below), it is the famously enigmatic last words of the braggart Armado in *Love's Labour's Lost* that perfectly summarize that strangely elated melancholy that still accompanies a play's final curtain: 'The words of Mercury are harsh after the songs of Apollo. You that way; we this way.'

Can this really be the end?

'But speak you on,' says the dying Edmund to Edgar in the final scene of *King Lear*, 'You look as you had something more to say' – one of a series of superfluously protracted exchanges in that profound meditation on human suffering by which its audience's 'theatrical endurance' somehow parallels the arduous trials of its characters.* When the end finally comes, it does so in the conventional form by which the play's blank verse yields, after the King's death, to the formal closure of a rhyming couplet. Except that the shared 'weight of this sad time' is distributed among its three shattered survivors and along four such couplets, each of which *might* bring down the curtain, but only the last of which – and at long last – does.

King Lear (1605), 5.3:

EDGAR.   He is gone indeed.

KENT. The wonder is he hath endur'd so long;
   He but usurp'd his life.

ALBANY. Bear them from hence. Our present business
   Is general woe. — Friends of my soul, you twain,
   Rule in this realm and the °gor'd state sustain.

KENT. I have a journey, sir, shortly to go;
   My master calls me, I must not say no.

---

* The phrase is from Stephen Booth's superlative essay 'On the Greatness of *King Lear*', in his *'King Lear', 'Macbeth', Indefinition, and Tragedy* (Yale, 1983), pp. 1–57.

EDGAR. The weight of this sad time we must obey,
    Speak what we feel, not what we ought to say.
    The oldest hath borne most; we that are young
    Shall never see so much, nor live so long.

Exeunt with a dead march.

The stop-and-start rhymes and rhythms of the ending of *King Lear* feel almost like a solemn parody of Bottom's over-indulgent death-scene as Pyramus ('Now am I dead, / Now am I fled...': see above, pp. 105–6). The Epilogue to *The Tempest* – the last that Shakespeare wrote, assuming that it was Fletcher who did the honours for *Henry VIII* and *The Two Noble Kinsmen* – achieves the very opposite effect. Audiences of Prospero's last speech are less likely to expect each of its couplets to prompt the 'hands' and 'breath' of their applause than to wonder whether the speaker, 'most faint', is going to make it to the next rhyme. Scholars remain divided over whether it is properly the fragility of the character or of the author that created him – and may even have played him – that seeps into the faltering trimeters of his farewell.

The Tempest (1612), Epilogue:

PROSPERO. Now my charms are all o'erthrown,
    And what strength I have's mine own,
    Which is most faint: now, 'tis true,
    I must be here confin'd by you,
    Or sent to Naples. Let me not,
    Since I have my dukedom got
    And pardon'd the deceiver, dwell
    In this bare island by your spell;
    But release me from my °bands
    With the help of your good hands:
    Gentle breath of yours my sails
    Must fill, or else my project fails,
    Which was to please. Now I °want
    Spirits to enforce, art to enchant,
    And my ending is despair,

Unless I be reliev'd by prayer,
Which °pierces so that it assaults
Mercy itself and frees all faults.
As you from °crimes would pardon'd be,
Let your °indulgence set me free.

Working somewhat like an emotional decompression chamber, the Epilogues of Shakespeare's plays debrief his
audiences into the social and financial realities of the trans-
action now coming to an end – 'to pray for the Queen' after
a performance at court, for example, or to 'beg the plaudit'
(or *seek the applause*) that will guarantee a repeat performance.
('Ay, but how if they do not clap their hands?' says the leading
actor to the company playwright, after rehearsing a particularly insipid Epilogue, in Marston's *Histriomastix*. 'No matter,
so they thump us not,' comes the pragmatic reply.) Likewise,
the real 'women' and 'beards' to which Rosalind refers in
hers, at the Globe, highlight their previous illusion (by an all-
male company, wearing artificial hair and make-up) in such
a way as to make us realize that 'her' Epilogue is – of course
and in fact – properly 'his':

As You Like It (1599–1600), Epilogue (in the public theatre):

ROSALIND. It is not the fashion to see the lady the
    Epilogue; but it is no more unhandsome than to see
    the lord the Prologue. If it be true that °good wine
    needs no bush, 'tis true that a good play needs no
    Epilogue; yet to good wine they do use good bushes,
    and good plays prove the better by the help of good
    Epilogues. What a °case am I in then, that am neither a
    good Epilogue nor cannot °insinuate with you in the
    behalf of a good play! I am not furnished like a beggar,
    therefore to beg will not become me: my way is to
    °conjure you, and I'll begin with the women. I charge
    you, O women, for the love you bear to men, to like as
    much of this play as please you. And I charge you, O
    men, for the love you bear to women (as I perceive by
    your simpering none of you hates them) that between

you and the women the play may please. If I were a woman I would kiss as many of you as had beards that pleased me, °complexions that liked me, and breaths that I defied not. And I am sure as many as have good beards, or good faces, or sweet breaths will for my kind offer, when I make curtsy, bid me farewell.

Exit.

'Still beginning in the ending'

Ever since its discovery in Cambridge University Library in 1975, a manuscript poem titled 'to yᵉ Q[ueen]. by yᵉ players 1598' has floated on the fringes of the Shakespeare canon. Since the Old-Style calendar began the new year on 25 March, rather than 1 January, the piece has been identified as an alternative Epilogue to be spoken at court – specifically at Richmond Palace at Shrovetide (18–20 February) 1599 – instead of either Puck's in *A Midsummer Night's Dream* or Rosalind's in *As You Like It.** The eighteen-line poem tactfully seeks to convert an ending into a new beginning for a now visibly ageing Queen Elizabeth – inverting the hour-glass, as it were, that Shakespeare's later Chorus of Time wields in *The Winter's Tale*. The full text of Marston's parody of a dreadful Epilogue supplies an effective précis: 'The glass is run, / Our play is done. / Hence time doth call, / We thank you all.' But did Shakespeare write this variant on the form?

A Court Epilogue (February 1599):

> As the dial hand °tells o'er
> The same hours it had before,
> Still beginning in the ending,
> °Circular account still lending,

* See James Shapiro, *1599: A Year in the Life of William Shakespeare* (Faber, 2005), pp. 84–7; and *As You Like It*, ed. Juliet Dusinberre (Arden Shakespeare, 2006), pp. 36–42, 349–54. (Both scholars describe their proposed addition of these lines to the end of each play as 'seamless'.)

So, most mighty Queen, we pray,
Like the dial day by day,
You may lead the seasons on,
Making new when old are gone;
That the babe which now is young
And hath yet no use of tongue
Many a Shrovetide here may bow
To that Empress I do now;
That the children of these lords,
Sitting at your council boards,
May be grave and agèd seen
Of her that was their fathers' Queen.
Once I wish this wish again,
Heaven subscribe it with 'Amen'.

Exeunt omnes

Shakespeare's earlier spokesman, Peter Quince, was aware of such conventions, closing *Pyramus and Thisbe* on a rhyme ('Come, blade, my breast imbrue! / And farewell, friends: / Thus Thisbe ends. / Adieu, adieu, adieu'), though he evidently also composed an Epilogue for it, which, in the event, remains unheard. For once sensitive to his aristocratic audience's impatience, Rosalind's fellow connoisseur of beards Nick Bottom offers a choice between 'seeing' Quince's Epilogue and 'hearing' the rustic dance of a 'Bergomask' – the latter option swiftly accepted by Duke Theseus as the most tactful way of curtailing the entire shambles.

A Midsummer Night's Dream (1595), 5.1:

BOTTOM. Will it please you to see the Epilogue, or to hear the Bergomask dance between two of our company?

THESEUS. No Epilogue, I pray you — for your play needs no excuse. Never excuse: for when the players are all dead, there need none to be blamed. Marry, if he that writ it had played Pyramus and hanged himself in

Thisbe's garter, it would have been a fine tragedy —
and so it is, truly; and very notably discharged. But
come, your Bergomask! Let your Epilogue alone.

In the play's first production, Theseus's command may have
deliberately been meant to showcase the accomplished
dancing skills of the actor playing Bottom – the company's
celebrated Clown (and founder member), Will Kemp. It has
certainly been argued that the originally published Epilogue
to *Henry IV, Part Two* is a garbled conflation of at least two
separate speeches – respectively by Will Kemp (flexing his
knees for a dance after playing Falstaff in the public theatre),
and by Will Shakespeare (embracing his role as principal
playwright, and bending his knees at court) – the same
distribution of labour as between Bottom's Bergomask and
Quince's Epilogue.

Henry IV, Part Two (1597–8), Epilogue (in the public theatre):

KEMP. If my tongue cannot entreat you to acquit me, will
   you command me to use my legs? and yet that were
   but light payment, to dance out of your debt. But a
   good conscience will make any possible satisfaction,
   and so would I. All the gentlewomen here have
   forgiven me; if the gentlemen will not, then the
   gentlemen do not agree with the gentlewomen —
   which was never seen before in such an assembly.

   One word more, I beseech you. If you be not too
   much cloyed with fat meat, our humble author will
   continue the story, with Sir John in it, and make you
   merry with fair Katherine of France: where, for
   anything I know, Falstaff shall die of a °sweat, unless
   already he be killed with your hard opinions; for
   °Oldcastle died a martyr, and this is not the man. My
   tongue is weary; when my legs are too, I will bid you
   good night.

Henry IV, Part Two (1597–8), Epilogue (at court):

SHAKESPEARE. First, my fear; then, my curtsy; last my speech. My fear is your displeasure; my curtsy, my duty; and my speech, to beg your pardons. If you look for a good speech now, you undo me, for what I have to say is of mine own making, and what indeed I should say will, I doubt, prove mine own marring. But to the purpose, and so to the venture.

Be it known to you, as it is very well, I was lately here in the end of a °displeasing play, to pray your patience for it, and to promise you a better. I meant indeed to pay you with this, which if like an ill venture it come unluckily home, I °break, and you, my gentle °creditors, lose. Here I promised you I would be, and here I commit my body to your mercies. °Bate me some and I will pay you some and, as most debtors do, promise you infinitely. And so I kneel down before you; but indeed, to pray for the Queen.

Following a typical Elizabethan play's final couplet, its '*Exeunt omnes*', the graceful farewell bestowed by its Epilogue, and the group dance by its cast, there remained one last coda by which it could take its leave – the positively final appearance of its Clown. The musical free-form of this solo performance, pioneered by the great comedian Richard Tarlton in the 1580s, and inherited by Will Kemp, was known as 'the Jig' – a sort of bawdy song-and-dance routine – or 'cinquepace of jests' – more recognizable from later music hall or vaudeville than 'legit' Shakespearean theatre. In fact, the two variant Epilogues from *Henry IV, Part Two* illustrate something of the same divergence. For in contrast to the practised mock-humility of the authorial voice ('If you look for a good speech now, you undo me, for what I have to say is of mine own making'), Kemp's dancing out of character to wish his fans 'good night' with a Jig must have broken the spell of the play's poignant last moments (the rejection of that other 'good knight' Jack Falstaff) with all the subtlety of Porky Pig's emergence at the end of Looney

Tunes cartoons – and with much the same message: 'Th-Th-Th-That's all Folks!'

And shortly afterwards, from Kemp's point of view, it was. Whoever it was that wrote it, Kemp's pre-Jig Epilogue supplies the Elizabethan equivalent of a 'trail', unique in the canon, which promises that 'our humble author will continue the story, with Sir John in it… for anything I know'. That airy disclaimer proved well founded. For by the time his 'humble author' *had* continued the story (in time perhaps for the company's transfer to the Globe in 1599), Kemp had made his own private farewells, to be replaced in the company by the subtler verbal wit – and singing voice – of Robert Armin. A Groucho Marx to Kemp's more physical Charlie Chaplin, it is generally accepted that Armin's roles included Touchstone in *As You Like It*, the Fool in *King Lear*, and Autolycus in *The Winter's Tale*, and his talents were foregrounded in the song – very much *not* a Jig – he sang as the forlorn Fool Feste at the end of *Twelfth Night*.

Twelfth Night (1601–2), 5.1:

FESTE.
When that I was and a little tiny boy,
    With hey, ho, the wind and the rain,
A foolish thing was but a toy,
    For the rain it raineth every day.

But when I came to man's estate,
    With hey, ho, the wind and the rain,
'Gainst knaves and thieves men shut their gate,
    For the rain it raineth every day.

But when I came, alas, to wive,
    With hey, ho, the wind and the rain,
By swaggering could I never thrive,
    For the rain it raineth every day.

But when I came unto my beds,
    With hey, ho, the wind and the rain,
°With toss-pots still had drunken heads,
    For the rain it raineth every day.

A great while ago the world begun,
   With hey, ho, the wind and the rain,
But that's all one, our play is done,
   And we'll strive to please you every day.

Exit.

The decline of the Jig seems to have coincided with a popular
trend for Epilogues in the early 1600s ('Th'Epilogue is now in
fashion, Prologues no more,' asserts the Chorus to an obscure
play called *The Birth of Hercules* in 1604), and it is no accident
that *Henry V* ended, not with a Jig, or even a Song, but with an
Epilogue – and in the altogether more high-minded form of a
sonnet, which advertised the entire sequence its 'bending
author' had now brought to a close. This closing message was
implicitly different: not 'Th-Th-Th-That's all Folks!', but
'W-W-W-Watch this Space!' And what a space it turned out to
be – from Ancient Rome and Elsinore, via Dover Beach and
Dunsinane, to Prospero's Island.

Henry V (1599), Epilogue:

CHORUS. Thus far, with rough and all-unable pen,
   Our bending author hath pursued the story,
   In °little room confining mighty men,
   °Mangling by starts the full course of their glory.
   Small time, but in that small most greatly liv'd
   This star of England: Fortune made his sword,
   By which the world's best garden he achiev'd,
   And of it left his son imperial lord.
   Henry the Sixth, in °infant bands crown'd King
   Of France and England, did this king succeed,
   Whose state so many had the managing,
   That they lost France and made his England bleed:
      Which oft our stage hath shown; and, for their sake,
      In your fair minds let this acceptance take.

Such literary self-consciousness prefigured the eventual collection of Shakespeare's plays in the 1623 First Folio – a
posthumous task, unhappily, following the premature extinction

of his 'muse of fire' in April 1616. The printer of Marlowe's
Tamburlaine, way back in 1590, at the outset of Shakespeare's
career, confessed to having 'purposely omitted and left out some
°fond and frivolous gestures, digressing (and in my poor opinion) far unmeet for the matter'. Heminge and Condell faced
similar decisions during the preparation of their monumental
First Folio edition, guaranteeing the plays' future afterlife –
around half had never previously been published – but also
monumentalizing their originally collective composition, from a
set of provisional and collaborative working scripts into a canon-
ical literary text. It is fitting that Hugh Holland's dedicatory
sonnet, placed immediately before the 'Catalogue of the several
Comedies, Histories, and Tragedies in this Volume', imagines
Shakespeare's death as a final exit from the world's stage – followed by a further Chorus (or *'nuncius'*) announcing their
endless revival: his eternal fame.

Hugh Holland, 'Upon the Lines and Life of the Famous
Scenic Poet, Master William Shakespeare' (1623):

> Those hands which you so clapp'd, go now and wring,
> You Britons brave: for done are Shakespeare's days!
> His days are done that made the °dainty plays
> Which made the Globe of heaven and earth to ring.
> Dried is that vein, dried is the Thespian spring,
> Turn'd all to tears, and °Phoebus clouds his rays.
> That corpse, that coffin, now °bestick those bays
> Which crown'd him poet first, then poets' king.
> If Tragedies might any Prologue have,
> All those he made would scarce make one to this,
> Where Fame (now that he gone is to the grave,
> Death's public tiring-house) the *nuncius* is.
>> For though his line of life went soon about,
>> The life yet of his lines shall never out.

... and it was all a dream

A decade or so after the publication of the Shakespeare First Folio – and a few years after its second edition – the Spanish dramatist Calderòn wrote a play whose title, *Life is a Dream*, might stand as a permanent motto for the thirty-six stories Heminge and Condell compiled, reflecting the full range of the *OED* definition of the word 'dream': '(*v.*, *obs.*) To make a musical or joyful noise... to form imaginary visions... (*n.*) A train of thought, images, or fancies passing through the mind... an object seen in a vision... an ideal or aspiration... a vision of the fancy... something of dreamlike beauty... (*adj.*) Such as one dreams of or longs to have; perfect.'

The Taming of a Shrew (1590), Epilogue:

> *Exeunt the* PLAYERS. *Then enter two bearing off* CHRISTOPHER SLY *in his own apparel again, and leave him where they found him, and then go out. Then enter the* °TAPSTER.

TAPSTER. Now that the darksome night is overpast,
And dawning day appears in crystal sky,
Now must I haste abroad. — But soft, who's this?
What, Sly? Oh, wondrous! Hath he lain here all night?
I'll wake him. I think he's starv'd by this,
But that his belly was so stuff'd with ale. —
What, how, Sly! Awake, for shame!

SLY (*waking*). Sim, gi's some more wine. What, 's all the players gone? Am not I a lord?

TAPSTER. A lord? °With a murrain! Come, art thou drunken still?

SLY. Who's this? Tapster? Oh Lord, sirrah, I have had the bravest dream tonight that ever thou heardst in all thy life.

TAPSTER. Ay, marry, but you had best get you home. For your wife will °course you for dreaming here tonight.

SLY. Will she? I know now how to tame a shrew: I dreamt upon it all this night till now, and thou hast waked me out

of the best dream that ever I had in my life. But I'll to my
wife presently, and tame her, too, an if she anger me —

TAPSTER. Nay, tarry, Sly, for I'll go home with thee,
And hear the rest that thou hast dreamt tonight.

Exeunt omnes.

A Midsummer Night's Dream (1595), Epilogue:

PUCK. If we shadows have offended,
Think but this, and all is °mended:
That you have but slumber'd here
While these visions did appear;
And this weak and idle theme,
No more yielding but a dream,
Gentles, do not reprehend:
If you pardon, we will °mend.
And, as I am an honest Puck,
If we have unearnèd luck
Now to scape the °serpent's tongue,
We will make amends ere long.
Else the Puck a liar call:
So good night unto you all.
Give me your hands, if we be friends,
And °Robin shall °restore amends.

The Tempest (1612), 4.1:

PROSPERO.   Be cheerful, sir,
Our revels now are ended. These our actors,
As I foretold you, were all spirits, and
Are melted into air, into thin air;
And like the °baseless fabric of this vision,
The cloud-capp'd towers, the gorgeous palaces,
The solemn temples, the great globe itself,
Yea, all which it inherit, shall dissolve,
And like this insubstantial pageant faded
Leave not a °rack behind. We are such stuff
As dreams are made on; and our little life
Is rounded with a sleep.

Glossary

abridgement   pastime, interlude

abstract and brief chronicles of the time   synopsis and condensed
    epitome of the age

Aeneas' tale to Dido   in Virgil's *Aeneid*, Aeneas relates the
    events of the fall of Troy to Dido, Queen of Carthage (as
    dramatized in Marlowe and Nashe's 1580s play of that
    name)

afford   permit, allow

aggravate   intensify (Bottom thinks it means the opposite:
    'moderate')

agree   i.e. agree financial terms

all long of you   all your fault

altitude of a chopine   height of an actor's platform-heeled shoe

an, an if   if

apology for that purpose   formal explanation (by a Chorus) to
    that effect

apprehend… comprehends   imagine… incorporates

Askance and strangely   In a distantly oblique or hostile manner

Asphaltis' lake   the bituminous tar-pits, or crude-oil fields,
    for which Babylon was famous

Assume the port of Mars   Adopt the bearing of the Roman god
    of war

at each   end on end

Ate   the Roman goddess of discord (pronounced *Ah-tay*)

Attest in little place a million   Signify vast multiplication (by the addition of a figure or a zero)

audients   listeners, members of the audience

bald crown   i.e. the baldness resulting from syphilis (or its treatment)

band-strings   collar-fastenings

bands   bondage, imprisonment

barmy   frothy, sticky

barren   mentally dull (*barren of new pride* = sterile of new invention)

baseless fabric   insubstantial material

Bate me some   Lessen the debt ('cut me some slack')

beget a temperance   acquire a moderation

bestick those bays   adorn with the laurel-crown of poetic achievement

bestowed   provided for, looked after

bill of properties   list of props

blindly in thine own opinion dost stand   stubbornly labour under a false impression

blocks   inert lumps

bourn   frontier, boundary

brake   thicket, clump

brand   stigma, mark of infamy (literally seared on to the flesh of criminals with a hot iron in the period)

brave   splendid, magnificent, richly clad (*bravely… trimm'd up* = richly decorated)

break   (1) face bankruptcy; (2) break my promise

Breaks scurril jests   Cracks subversive jokes

brief   summary, inventory, docket

brisky juvenile   sprightly lad

brute part of him to kill so capital a calf   brutal action of his to kill such an utter fool (punning on 'Brutus', *part* = 'role', 'Capitol', and a style of public butchery of meat)

bully   fine fellow (term of endearment)

but   except for, but for

butter-firkin   cask of butter

Buzz, buzz!   usually explained as an expression of contempt for old news; but perhaps also a sardonic parody of an audience's expectation (cf. 'the buzzing pleasèd multitude', p. 162)

By'r la'kin   By Our Ladykin (i.e. Mary, mother of Christ)

caliver   a light-calibred musket

Cambyses' vein   the old-fashioned style associated with the ranting style of the tyrant of Thomas Preston's 1569 eponymous play

camomile, the more it is trodden... the sooner it wears   a direct parody of a characteristically laboriously formal rhetorical metaphor in John Lyly's *Euphues* (1589): 'Though the camomile, the more it is trodden and pressed down, the more it spreadeth, yet the violet the oftener it is handled and touched, the sooner it withereth and decayeth...'

carbuncles   crimson-coloured gemstones

case   predicament

casement   hinged window

casques   helmets

caviare to the general   too good for the unrefined tastes of its audience (cf. 'pearls before swine')

Cephalus... Procris   an ill-fated couple from Ovid's *Metamorphoses*: falsely suspecting her husband Cephalus of adultery, Procris secretly follows him when he goes hunting – but when she rustles in the bushes, Cephalus kills her with a spear. In Shakespeare's script, Bottom mispronounces them as 'Shafalus' and 'Procrus'.

change your place   move to somewhere else

chime a-mending, with terms unsquar'd   out-of-tune bells, jarringly ill-fitting

chopped   coarse, callused (as in 'horny-handed sons of toil')

cinquepace   an energetic dance

ciphers to this great account   meaningless noughts in our computed sum

Circular account still lending   Forever bestowing its endless circuit

cits   tradesman

cleave the general ear   present a shattering effect to all members of the audience

clerks   scholars, officials

clew   ball of thread

closes with you in this consequence   confides in you to the following extent

coarse-frieze capacities   vulgar intellects

cock   dinghy (the rowing-boat towed behind a ship)

codpiece   the padded flap in the crotch of a man's breeches (often set with decorative pins, or *points*)

commonty   a portmanteau word combining 'comedy' and 'commodity' (= merchandise)

compass... farthingale   circumference... hooped skirt

complexions that liked me... that I defied not   appearances that appealed to me... which I didn't entirely despise

con   memorize, learn by heart

concord of this discord   rationale for this nonsense

condole   lament

Confederate season, else no creature seeing   With the opportunity presenting itself, and with no one else present to witness it

congée   bow

conjure   entreat, bewitch

Content   'Agreed', 'So be it'

coted   overtook

counterpane   the counterfoil of a legal contract

course   (*vb*) chase you with blows, chastise

cracked within the ring   broken as to its formerly higher pitch (as an illegally clipped coin is withdrawn from circulation)

creditors   investors

cried in the top of mine   authoritatively excelled my own

crimes   sins

crowkeeper   scarecrow

cuffs   blows, fisticuffs

cullison   badge

dainty   delightful, esteemed, worthy (*dainty of his worth* = complacent about his own value)

Damon   in Greek mythology the model of an ideal friend

deck   clothe, adorn

defect   flaw, fault (Bottom's flawed attempt at 'effect')

deficient sight   dizzying vision

defied not   didn't entirely flinch from

dejected 'haviour of the visage   downcast facial expression

descant   set of (musical) variations

despite   scorn, disdain

device   performance, production

disfigure   deface (Quince means *figure* = 'impersonate', 'represent')

displeasing play   see *Oldcastle died a martyr*

dole   sorrow, grief

do you   (*imperative*) 'you should'

drabbing   whoring, associating with harlots

dropsy   a disease of water-retention (*the dropsy drown this fool* = may this idiot be struck down by disease)

easy standings   (1) comfortable standing room; (2) discreetly
satisfied male desires

eight-and-six... eight-and-eight   Quince suggests a standard
ballad metre ('De-dum, de-dum, de-dum, de-dum / De-
dum, de-dum, de-dum, / De-dum, de-dum, de-dum,
de-dum, / De-dum de-dum, de-dum'), which Bottom
eagerly – and vainly – seeks to improve ('De-dum, de-
dum, de-dum, de-dum / De-dum, de-dum, de-dum,
de-dum, de-dum...'). In the event, though, Quince writes
this Prologue in five-beat pentameters (see pp. 102–3).

eke   (*archaic*) also

end   intention

end his part in peace   be allowed to finish his lines without
interruption

entertain... at a low rate   cheaply employ

equipage   hierarchical procession

Eripha   in Greek mythology, a horse owned by a thwarted
lover, and buried with him. Hence *that old trot* = old
woman, hag, 'old trout'.

Ercles... tear a cat... make all split   i.e. Hercules (the superhero
of Roman myth)... yowlingly emote... present a totally
shattering effect

escoted   maintained, employed

every mother's son   each one of us

falchion   sabre

falling sickness   epilepsy (a term which Cassius pretends to
take literally – he, Brutus, and Casca 'falling' as Caesar
rises)

Fates   i.e. the Three Classical sister-goddesses who spin,
draw out, and cut the individual threads of our lives

fellowship in a cry of players   shareholder's stake in a company
of actors

figure   rhetorical device, stylistic flourish (*by a figure* =
metaphorically speaking)

fill up rooms in fair and formal shapes   occupy stage-boxes in guise of gentlemen

fire of grace   divine influence channelled by monarchs

fitted   cast

flat unraisèd spirits   inert and uninspired efforts of our actors

foil and target   sword and shield

fond and frivolous gestures   foolish and trivial episodes

form and pressure   shape and character (*forms… pressures past* = influential ideas… previous impressions)

free   innocent

frighted with false fire   scared by the bang of a firework

fruitful   copious

fusty stuff   stale bombast

gather wind by firking up their breeches   recover their breath by pausing to hitch up their trousers

general   (*n.*) general public, common populace; (*adj.*) universal

give the foil, / Save them that yield, and spare where they may spoil   supply the discrepancy, / Forgive those who confess their faults, rather than condemning them

Give o'er   Abandon

God's-lid   God's eye-lid, often elided to ''Slid' (a flippant oath)

Golden Fleece   in Greek mythology, the sacred prize captured by Jason and his Argonauts

good wine needs no bush   i.e., a decent product requires no advertising (from the traditional inn-sign of a *bush* – as in 'down at the old Bull and Bush')

Gor'd mine own thoughts   Defiled my innermost feelings and purposes

gor'd state sustain   support and help to heal the wounded commonwealth *got with a look… lost again with a wink*   won over with an amorous glance… but lost in the blink of an eye (to another's winning glance)

greater time   older years

groat   fourpenny piece

grounded   (1) established, firmly established; (2) standing on the ground of the playhouse

groundlings   frequenters of the theatre 'yard', who stood in front of the stage, rather than paying more for a seat in the galleries.

grow to a point come to a conclusion

The Gull's Hornbook   'An Idiot's Guide', 'A Simpleton's Handbook'

halt   go lame (and lose rhythm)

harlotry   (*adj.*) trashy, tawdry (possibly one of Mistress Quickly's malapropisms)

have audience   be allowed to be heard

heaviness   (1) weight; (2) grief, sorrow

Hecate's ban   the curse – or poison ('bane') – of the goddess of witchcraft

Hecuba   the Queen of Troy, whose eighteen sons by King Priam died with him during the Greeks' sack of the city

Hercules   the Roman superhero, whose Twelve Labours are still famous (*Hercules in minority… strangling a snake* = a reference to his feat of killing a serpent as he lay in his crib; *Hercules Furens* = a tragedy by Seneca, in which the hero is driven mad, and kills his own children)

holds his countenance   keeps a straight face; stays in character

holp   helped

honesty   the common garden plant *lunaria* (carrying the obvious moral sense)

horrid suit of the camp   rough military dress

hose stocking (*His youthful hose, well sav'd, a world too wide /
For his shrunk shank* = the stockings the young man once
thriftily put aside no longer fits his withered limbs in old
age)

Hyrcanian beast i.e. the (famously savage) tiger from
modern-day Turkmenistan

ill-favour'd ugly, unattractive

imbrue pierce, bloodily stab

in cue in his proper disposition

in snuff (1) i.e. a candle in need of trimming or snuffing;
(2) angry, liable to 'flare up' with rage

in your allowance by your own admission

incontinent immediately

indifferently pretty well, to a large extent

indulgence favourable reward; remission from punishment

infant bands swaddling clothes

insinuate curry favour

intend express, profess, pretend

interlocutions conversational exchanges

*It is as dangerous to read his name at a play-door as a printed bill on
a plague-door* That playwright is box-office poison – as
fatal to our hopes as a set of printed mortality figures
posted up on the sealed door of a household infested by
plague (usually marked by a cross)

Jack of the clock-house literally the clockwork manikin that
struck the bell of a church clock; so here either in
reference to Belch's status as the company's leader (and
timekeeper); or disparagingly in reference to his age.
Belch recasts Posthaste as 'Slowpace' for being late, and
threatens to fine him a shilling.

jew (*obscure*) jewel, juvenile, Jew

Johannes factotum jack-of-all-trades

joint-stool   crudely made chair

journeymen   hired hands, inexperienced craftsmen

Jove   the Roman king of the gods

Juno... Mercury... Jove   in Roman mythology, the queen of the gods, the messenger of the gods, and the king of the gods

knell   death-knell, the tolling bell at a funeral

late innovation   recent troubles

lath   plywood

Leander... Hero   Ovid's *Heroides* tells how Leander of Abydos so loved Hero of Sestos that every night he swam across the stretch of water dividing them (the Hellespont), guided by a lamp on top of Hero's house. One night the lamp blew out, Leander drowned, and Hero killed herself on finding his beached corpse. In Shakespeare's script, Bottom mispronounces the first as 'Limander', and Flute says 'Helen' instead of 'Hero'.

lenten entertainment   niggardly welcome, lukewarm reception

lief   prefer (*I had as lief* = I would be just as happy if)

lime   cement

little room   a small space (perhaps punning on the literal meaning of *stanza*)

loam... rough-cast   moistened clay and straw... sand-and-gravel mixture

longs   belongs

lovers   loving subjects

made   financially secure

make my play   score (by winning the game and winning your hand)

Malevole in Folio... Jeronimo in Decimo-Sexto   (in reference to standard book-sizes) the hero of *The Malcontent* in expanded form... the hero of Kyd's *Spanish Tragedy* in a compressed version

Mangling by starts   Distorting by their episodic nature

mark   note, pay attention to

mark of favour   detail of appearance

May be grave and agèd seen / Of her that was their fathers' Queen
   May be seen in their old age by her that was also Queen to
   their fathers

meaning   intention

Mechanic slaves   Working-class rogues

meet   fitting, appropriate

Meleager and the boar   in Classical mythology, Meleager of
   Calydon organized the hunt for a monstrous marauding
   boar; Theseus was among the hunting party.

mend   improve, do better (*mended* = remedied)

merry gamester   (1) jocular prankster; (2) tipsy lecher

miching mallico   stealthy villainy

milked unto you   spoon-fed to you

modesties   collective discretion

modesty… cunning   restraint… skill

motley   the multicoloured costume of a court Fool or stage
   Jester (*made myself a motley to the view* = presented myself
   as a public Fool; *motley coat guarded with yellow* = that
   costume, traditionally trimmed or hemmed in yellow)

Murder thy breath   simulate being 'choked up' with emotion

muse   (*vb*) wonder, consider

naught   indecent, 'naughty'

Ninus   the founder of the Babylonian city of Nineveh
   (where the action of *Pyramus and Thisbe* is set)

noise of targets   clash of swords on shields

nuptial   wedding

O lente lente currite noctis equi   'Slowly, you horses of the night,
   run slowly': a line from Ovid's *Amores*, in which the
   speaker wishes to protract his night of sexual bliss

obscenely   properly 'offensively', but Bottom's odd mistake for either 'seemly' (= fitting) or 'obscurely' (= privately)

O'ercharg'd   Overloaded (as of a firearm or a burden)

o'erdoing Termagant; it out-Herods Herod   out-blustering the impersonation in old plays of a savage pagan god and the biblical King Herod (who ordered the Massacre of the Innocents after the birth of Christ)

o'ersizèd with coagulate gore   coated with clotted blood

o'ertook in's rouse… falling out at   drunkenly overcome… quarrelling over

o'er-wrested seeming   overwrought characterization

Oldcastle died a martyr   a reference to the scandal that had erupted around *Henry IV, Part One*, where Falstaff's surname had originally been 'Oldcastle' – to the displeasure of that executed fifteenth-century nobleman's descendants

on hazard   at the mercy of chance, at risk

on the bow hand   wide of the mark, barking up the wrong tree

opinion that we bring / To make that only true we now intend   our known reputation for fulfilling our promises

ordinary   chop-house, pie-shop

organ   means, instrument

over-eyeing   observing too closely

pageants   mimics, parodies, burlesques

pajock   peacock (the word 'ass' is expected by the rhyme)

pantaloon   an old man (defined by the baggy trousers he wears)

pap   breast

paramour… paragon   sexual mistress… supreme exemplar

parcel   company

pard   leopard

parlous   shrewd, dangerous, hazardous

party in converse... sound   interlocutor... take the measure of

pass   (*n.*) passage, voyage; (*vb*) pass muster, gain approval

peaking pageanter   aspiring playmaker

Pentecost   the festival of Whitsun (when may-games, morality plays, and other theatrical spectacles were performed)

person   bodily figure

Phibbus   i.e. *Phoebus* (whose 'car' was the chariot of the sun)

Phoebe, Flora, or the Huntress   the Greek goddess of the Moon (Diana), the Roman goddess of flowers, and the Roman Diana (the goddess of hunting)

Phoebus   Apollo, the Greek god of the sun (*the young Phoebus fanning* = wafting the morning sunlight like a fan)

phrase of war   military jargon

pierces so that it assaults / Mercy itself and frees all faults   so penetrates the heart of divine grace with its force that all is forgiven

plaudities   applause, critical acclaim

pluck'd   pulled down

plum-broth and marrow   essential nutritious core

poetic furies   dauntingly inspired spirits; furious poets

points   (1) details; (2) the tagged laces of a costume; (3) punctuation marks

posy   inscription, motto

pouch   money-bag, purse

preferr'd   presented, brought in evidence

prenominate   aforementioned

Priam   the King of Troy

Proh Deum! Medius Fidius!   (*Latin*) 'Alas, by God! God help me!'

project   intention; business venture; experiment

promontory   (*literally*) a piece of land jutting out into the sea; (*figuratively*) the extended stage of a public theatre

provincial roses... razed shoes   French-style rosettes... fashionably slashed shoes

'P.S.', 'O.P.'   prompt side (stage left), opposite prompt (stage right)

puppet   powerless object of display or impersonation (as in a modern 'puppet government'); gawdy simulacrum

put-down stews   suppressed brothels ('The stews once stood where now playhouses stand,' reads John Davies's own explanatory note in the margin – though the suppression was evidently incomplete)

Pyrrhus   the son of the Greek hero Achilles, one of the number smuggled into Troy in the 'ominous' Wooden Horse, that led to the city's destruction

quail   subject, overpower, annihilate

quality   the rank or standing of an occupation, especially used of actors

Quicken with kissing   Let me revive you by my kissing you

rack   wisp of cloud

rail   verbally abuse (*railing... reigning* = abusing... ruling: punning on 'gushing... raining')

rare   splendid, excellent (*drawn so rarely* = so vividly depicted)

receives a brand   is stigmatized (as with a branding iron on criminals)

relative   pertinent, immediate, relevant

restore amends   be mutually grateful in return

ripe   ready, prepared

Robin   i.e. Robin Goodfellow, another name for the mischievous hobgoblin Puck

robustious periwig-pated fellow   boisterous, bewigged actor

rude coil   clamorous fuss

russet, tissue   coarse cloth, rich finery

sable... gules... trick'd   black... red... patterned (heraldic terms)

sack   white wine (*vin sec*)

Sail seas in cockles, have and wish but for't   Travel the ocean in a tiny shell by merely wishing it so

sallets in the lines to make the matter savoury... matter in the phrase sauciness in the material to make it emptily sensational... stylistic content

samphire   the salty marine plant that grows on cliffs (hence the 'dreadful trade' of harvesting it)

Sans   Without (from the French, but pronounced to rhyme with *pans*)

saucy lictors... strumpets... scald rhymers... quick comedians insolent officials... whores... scabby balladeers... improvising actors

saws and modern instances   moral precepts and recent legal precedents

scaped   escaped, evaded, got away with anything less than

scene individable or poem unlimited... the law of writ and the liberty plays obeying the Three Unities (of Time, Place, and Action) or deliberately ignoring them... whether obeying such formal literary constraints or experimenting without them

sconce... breach... convoy   fortification... the gap in defences opened up by artillery... armed escort (military terms)

screw'd   wrenched

scrip   text, script

seesaw sack-a-down, like a sawyer   i.e. the artificial gesturing – as predictable as that of one sawing wood – that is the mark of the amateur actor

serpent's tongue   i.e, the hiss of an audience's displeasure

shifts extempore   improvised routines

shiver'd   shattered

shrouds   sail-ropes

sinew and the forehand of our host   foremost strength in our
    army

sinister   left

Sisters Three   see *Fates*

snag   trunk, stump, log

Soto   Evidently the name of a character ('a farmer's eldest
    son') performed by the Second Player in a production that
    the Lord remembers him in

spent their wits   exhausted their inventive imagination

stand for seed… put in   be held in reserve for future growth
    (with a bawdy pun on 'maintain their erections')… made
    a bid

state   throne of state

stayed for   waited for

steaded   benefited, assisted

still   continually, forever (*still answer nay, and take it* =
    constantly protest, then submit; *still taught* = be
    continually spoon-fed one's lines)

strength's abundance   excess of feeling

sucking dove   another of Bottom's confusions: he means
    either the proverbially mild 'sucking lamb' or the 'sitting
    dove' nesting her eggs

suit of jests   organized collection – or 'suite' – of gags; set of
    catchphrases

sweat   fever, whether of plague or venereal disease

table   notebook

taffeta   the silken material used for exotic masks

tag-rag people   riff-raff

tapster   publican, barman

tar   incite, provoke

tarry at a stand   remain unable to proceed

tear a passion   mangle a set-piece speech

tediosity and disinsanity   tiresome bother and madness (the first of Gerald's tiresomely bothersome and mad circumlocutions in this speech)

tells   counts

tent him to the quick   probe him to the sensitive marrow

Terence   Publius Terentius Afer (c. 190–159 BC), Roman comic dramatist

'Then came each actor on his ass —'   one of *Hamlet*'s obscurer allusions, tentatively identified as a fragment of a lost ballad (generally the last resort of a flummoxed editor)

Then know that I as Snug the joiner am / A lion fell, nor else no lion's dam   So understand that, insofar as I am Snug the joiner, I am a fierce lion, but in no other way am I the mother of all lions

thread and thrum   the lengthways 'warp' of a piece of woven cloth, and the tufted pieces remaining when the finished piece of weaving is cut off from the loom

Thy topless deputation he puts on   He parodies your supreme agency

tickle o' the sear   prone to explode in laughter (as of the hair-trigger of a gun)

tickle-brain   a type of strong ale (with the sense of an over-sensitive susceptibility)

trace   (1) follow in my footsteps; (2) tread a dance measure

transported   kidnapped, carried off, spirited away

tricks   characteristics, abilities, skills

tristful   (archaic) sorrowful, sad

truant   negligent practitioner

truchman   interpreter, intermediary

Typhon   in Greek mythology a monstrous giant associated with earthquakes and volcanoes *unbreath'd*   inexperienced, unexercised

understanding   (1) critically intelligent; (2) positioned immediately before the stage

unnumber'd idle pebble chafes   surges on to the inert and innumerably pebbled shore

unstaid   immodest

valanced... beard   fringed, edged, i.e. with a beard – hence Hamlet's pun on *beard* (*vb*) = defy, challenge

vaunt and firstlings of those broils   preliminary skirmishes of this war

vent   (*n.*) aperture; (*vb*) express, exhale, proclaim

veriest antic   greatest buffoon

viol da gamba   a cello-like stringed instrument

visage wann'd   face went pale

wagging   trembling

want   lack

warm   hard-working

warrant your honour   assure you, sir

'Was this the face —'   the stammering actor is quoting from Marlowe's *Doctor Faustus*: 'Was this the face that launch'd a thousand ships / And burnt the topless towers of Ilium?'

weeds   garments, items of clothing

ween   believe, imagine, suppose

wildfowl   bird (Bottom means 'wild animal')

With a murrain!   'The hell you are!' (*murrain* = pestilence)

With toss-pots still had drunken heads   The same hangovers afflicted me as any other drunkard (*toss-pot* = one who drains a tankard of drink)

Select Bibliography

Leeds Barroll, *Politics, Plague, and Shakespeare's Theater: The Stuart Years* (Cornell University Press, 1991)

Julian Bowsher and Pat Miller, *The Rose and the Globe – Playhouses of Shakespeare's Bankside, Southwark: Excavations 1988–91* (Museum of London, 2009)

Charles Boyce, *Shakespeare: A–Z of his Life and Works* (Roundtable Press, 1990)

Douglas Bruster and Robert Weimann, *Prologues to Shakespeare's Theatre* (Routledge, 2004)

Tarnya Cooper, ed., *Searching for Shakespeare* (National Portrait Gallery, 2006)

Michael Dobson and Stanley Wells, eds, *The Oxford Companion to Shakespeare* (Oxford University Press, 2001)

Katherine Duncan-Jones, *Shakespeare: An Ungentle Life* (Methuen Drama, 2010)

——————, *Shakespeare: Upstart Crow to Sweet Swan, 1592–1623* (Methuen Drama, 2011)

Lukas Erne, *Shakespeare as Literary Dramatist* (Cambridge University Press, 2003)

Jonathan and Moira Field, eds, *The Methuen Book of Theatre Verse* (Methuen Drama, 1991)

R.A. Foakes, ed., *Henslowe's Diary*, 2nd edition (Cambridge University Press, 2002)

Germaine Greer, *Shakespeare* (Past Masters series, Oxford University Press, 1986)

W.W. Greg, *Two Elizabethan Stage Abridgements: 'The Battle of Alcazar' & 'Orlando Furioso'* (Malone Society, 1923)

David Grote, *The Best Actors in the World: Shakespeare and his Acting Company* (Greenwood Press, 2002)

Andrew Gurr, *Playgoing in Shakespeare's London*, 3rd edition (Cambridge University Press, 2004)

Grace Ioppolo, *Dramatists and their Manuscripts in the Age of Shakespeare, Jonson, Middleton and Heywood: Authorship, Authority and the Playhouse* (Routledge, 2006)

Scott McMillin, 'Middleton's Theatres', in *Thomas Middleton: The Collected Works*, gen. ed. Gary Taylor and John Lavagnino (Clarendon Press, 2007), pp. 74–87

Dieter Mehl, *The Elizabethan Dumb Show: The History of a Dramatic Convention* (Methuen, 1965)

Charles Nicholl, *The Lodger: Shakespeare on Silver Street* (Allen Lane, 2007)

Michael Pennington, *Sweet William: Twenty Thousand Hours with Shakespeare* (Nick Hern Books, 2012)

Carol Chillington Rutter, ed., *Documents of the Rose Playhouse*, revised edition (Revels Plays Companion Library, Manchester University Press, 1999)

S. Schoenbaum, *William Shakespeare: A Documentary Life* (Oxford University Press, 1975)

James Shapiro, *1599: A Year in the Life of William Shakespeare* (Faber, 2005)

Tiffany Stern, *Documents of Performance in Early Modern England* (Cambridge University Press, 2009)

Simon Trussler, *The Faber Pocket Guide to Elizabethan and Jacobean Drama* (Faber, 2006)

Stanley Wells, *Shakespeare For All Time* (Macmillan, 2002)

Epigraph Sources

p. xi   Stephen Sondheim, *Frogs* (1974).

p. 1   Peter Motteux, Prologue to George Farquhar's *The Inconstant* (1702).

p. 1   Noël Coward, revised Prologue (1951) to *Conversation Piece* (1934).

p. 27   Joseph Addison, *The Playhouse* (c. 1700).

p. 27   Oscar Wilde, *Lord Arthur Savile's Crime* (1891).

p. 47   Anon., *The Prompter* (1810).

p. 47   *North by Northwest* (1959), written by Ernest Lehman, directed by Alfred Hitchcock.

p. 67   John O'Keefe, 'Wilde: Prompter to Covent Garden Theatre' (1826).

p. 67   W.B. Yeats, 'The Circus Animals' Desertion' (*Last Poems and Two Plays*, Cuala Press, 1939).

p. 97   Paul Valéry, '*Toujours nous sommes interrompus, jamais nous ne sommes achevés*', Introduction to La Fontaine, *Adonis* (1921).

p. 109   John Keats to Benjamin Bailey, 13 March 1818.

p. 109   Howard Dietz, 'That's Entertainment', *The Band Wagon* (1952).

p. 127   Sarah Siddons, Drury Lane Theatre, 10 October 1782, in Thomas Campbell, *Life of Mrs Siddons* (2nd edition, 1839).

p. 127   Marc Norman and Tom Stoppard, *Shakespeare in Love* (1999).

p. 145   William Congreve, Prologue to *The Double-Dealer* (1693).

p. 145   Stephen Sondheim, *Frogs* (2004 revival).

p. 173   William Makepeace Thackeray, 'The End of the Play' (1848).

p. 173   Walter Ralegh, 'On the Life of Man' (*c*. 1614).

Index of Works Cited